Grief

Mike Leigh's plays include: *Bleak Moments* (Open Space), *Wholesome Glory* (Royal Court Theatre Upstairs), *The Silent Majority* (Bush), *Babies Grow Old* (RSC), *Abigail's Party*, *Ecstasy*, *Goose-Pimples* and *Smelling a Rat* (Hampstead), *Greek Tragedy* (Belvoir Street, Sydney, Edinburgh Festival and Stratford East), *It's a Great Big Shame!* (Stratford East), *Two Thousand Years* (National Theatre). TV films: *Hard Labour*, *Nuts in May*, *The Kiss of Death*, *Who's Who*, *Grown-Ups*, *Home Sweet Home*, *Meantime*, *Four Days in July*, *A Sense of History*. TV studio plays: *The Permissive Society*, *Knock for Knock*, *Abigail's Party*. Radio play: *Too Much of a Good Thing*. Feature films: *Bleak Moments*, *The Short and Curlies*, *High Hopes*, *Life is Sweet*, *Naked*, *Secrets and Lies*, *Career Girls*, *Topsy-Turvy*, *All or Nothing*, *Vera Drake*, *Happy-Go-Lucky*, *Another Year*.

MIKE LEIGH

Grief

ff

faber and faber

First published in 2011
by Faber and Faber Limited
74–77 Great Russell Street, London WC1B 3DA

Typeset by Country Setting, Kingsdown, Kent CT14 8ES
Printed in England by CPI Group (UK) Ltd, Croydon CR0 4YY

A CIP record for this book
is available from the British Library

ISBN 978-0-571-28302-6

2 4 6 8 10 9 7 5 3 1

Grief was first performed in the Cottlesloe auditorium of the National Theatre, London, on 21 September 2011. The cast was as follows:

Dorothy Lesley Manville
Victoria Ruby Bentall
Edwin Sam Kelly
Hugh David Horovitch
Gertrude Marion Bailey
Muriel Wendy Nottingham
Maureen Dorothy Duffy

Director Mike Leigh
Designer Alison Chitty
Lighting Designer Paul Pyant
Music Gary Yershon
Sound Designer John Leonard

Characters

Dorothy

Victoria

Edwin

Hugh

Gertrude

Muriel

Maureen

The action takes place in the drawing room
of Dorothy's house in a leafy West London suburb.
An ample and comfortable Edwardian semi.

Time: between early winter 1957 and autumn 1958.

GRIEF

Setting

A bay window, with nets and curtains.
Parquet floor, a large, quality rug. Tasteful furniture.
Some antiques, some art deco. A sofa, an armchair,
a Georgian wooden chair with arms. Side tables, lamps.
Bookshelves (Penguins, bound classics). A sideboard,
on which is a vase of flowers and a large, silver tray
of sherry and whisky decanters, with their appropriate
glasses. A sewing box and a sewing basket are near the
armchair, near which are usually copies of women's
magazines, Picture Post *and* Illustrated, *now strewn*
untidily about the floor. A telephone can be seen on
the hall table. Radio, radiogram and television
cannot be seen, and do not figure in the action.

Scene and costume changes should be accomplished
as swiftly as possible.

SCENE ONE

A Monday morning in October.
Lights up. Dorothy comes downstairs and enters the room. She is hesitant and nervous. She picks up her spectacles and a couple of magazines. She goes towards the door. Maureen enters, tying up her apron. Pause.

Maureen Where do you want me to start?

Dorothy Oh. Em . . . I don't know.

Maureen In here? (*She looks round the room.*)

Dorothy Well, you could start upstairs, if you like.

Maureen I don't mind.

Dorothy Well, em . . . Hazel used to do downstairs first. Then she'd do the bedrooms and bathroom. Then the hall, stairs and landing. And she'd finish off in the kitchen.

Maureen That'll do. (*She proceeds to clear up.*)

Maureen crosses past Dorothy to the armchair table. Dorothy moves in front of her.

Dorothy (*apologetically*) Oh . . . handbag.

She retrieves her handbag from the floor beside the armchair and moves towards the door. Maureen holds up a cup and saucer.

Maureen Are you finished with this?

Dorothy Oh, yes. It's just my Bournvita cup from last night. A little nightcap.

3

*Dorothy goes out to the kitchen. Maureen collects a
sherry glass and a whisky glass from a side table, and
goes out. Dorothy returns. She takes a cigarette from
a silver cigarette box and lights it with the table lighter.
She hovers.*

*Maureen comes in, picks up a waste-paper basket,
and leaves.*

*Dorothy hovers nervously by the window, smoking.
She suddenly closes the lid of her sewing box.*

*Maureen returns with the waste-paper basket. She
proceeds to dust the ornaments on top of the bookshelf.*

Dorothy Have you had to come far?

Maureen Only Hounslow.

Dorothy Oh, yes, that's . . . em . . . near the London
Airport, isn't it?

Maureen It is, aye. Too near.

Pause.

Dorothy Are you from Ireland?

Maureen Aye. From Donegal.

Dorothy Oh, really? Yes, my brother and I had a nanny
from, um . . . oh – Letterkenny.

Maureen I meant to tell you, I have a week's holidays
booked at Christmas. I'm going home from the Saturday
to the Saturday. So I won't be about on the Monday or
the Friday.

Dorothy Oh, I see. I'm sorry, I didn't . . . I'm not quite
sure on which day Christmas falls this year.

Maureen Wednesday.

Dorothy Gosh. Well, we shall just have to make do
without you, won't we?

Maureen You will, aye. Will I be getting paid Fridays?

Dorothy Oh, yes, of course.

She turns to leave.

Maureen Are you not going out?

Dorothy Er, no . . . I wasn't planning to. I don't normally . . .

Maureen is dusting a framed photograph of a man.

Maureen Is that your husband?

She puts it back on the bookshelf.

Dorothy Yes, my late husband.

Maureen Was he killed in the war?

Dorothy Yes, he was, actually.

Maureen Sorry for your troubles.

Pause.

Dorothy Well, I'll let you get on.

Maureen Grand.

Dorothy leaves. Maureen carries on dusting.
Fade lights.

SCENE TWO

That afternoon. Dusk.
Lights up. Dorothy is sitting in her armchair knitting.
She stops, takes off her spectacles, and massages her
forehead. Then she gets up, turns on several lamps, and
proceeds to draw the curtains. As she does so, she waves
to somebody outside. We hear the front door. Dorothy
opens the door to the hall.

Victoria appears. She is wearing her school uniform and carries a satchel.

Dorothy Hello, darling.

Victoria Hello, Mummy.

Dorothy Have you been in detention?

Victoria Of course I've been in detention.

She hangs up her coat in the hall.

Dorothy What was it for this time?

Victoria The usual, Mummy.

She comes into the room, and sits on the sofa. Pause.

Dorothy Well, perhaps you should try a little harder to get your homework in promptly. (*Pause.*) I've been gasping for a cup of tea, but I thought I'd wait until you came home. Would you like a nice cup of tea?

Victoria Yes please, Mummy.

Dorothy sets off for the kitchen; she stops in the doorway.

Dorothy Oh, and some ginger cake . . . ?

Victoria does not reply. Dorothy goes to the kitchen. Pause. Victoria sighs. Dorothy returns.

The kettle's on.

She sits in the armchair.

How was your day?

Pause.

Oh, did you see Mary?

Victoria Yes, of course.

Dorothy Did she say that she saw me?

Victoria Yes.

Dorothy What did she say?

Victoria She said she saw you.

Dorothy Very nice-looking young man she was with. Is he a relative?

Victoria Don't be silly, Mummy.

Dorothy Gosh. I would have thought she was a bit young for that sort of thing.

Victoria She's exactly the same age as me.

Dorothy Yes, darling – that's my point. And she certainly wasn't smoking.

Victoria So what?

Dorothy Well, you told me that your friend smoked. And all I'm saying is, that when I saw her standing outside that coffee bar, she wasn't smoking.

Victoria She doesn't smoke every, every second of the day, for goodness sake.

Pause. Dorothy gets up.

Dorothy Well . . .

Victoria Did the new cleaner come?

Dorothy Oh, yes – she's very nice.

Victoria Did she go into my room?

Dorothy Yes, of course she went into your room, darling – she has to clean.

Victoria I hope she didn't move anything.

Dorothy I'm sure she didn't.

Victoria She better not.

> *Dorothy exits to the kitchen. Pause. Then Victoria gets up, collects her satchel from the hall, and goes upstairs. Dorothy returns, looks at the empty room, and exits to the kitchen.*
> *Fade lights.*

SCENE THREE

A little later.
> *We hear the front door opening. Edwin enters. He is wearing his hat and coat. He glances round the room. Then he goes out, and returns after a few moments without his hat and coat. He is carrying a book and a newspaper, which he puts on a side table by the sofa. He sits on the sofa.*
> *Pause. Enter Dorothy, wearing her apron.*

Dorothy Oh – goodness me! I didn't hear you come in.

Edwin Hello.

Dorothy How are you? A bit tired?

Edwin Just a little, yes.

Dorothy You poor old thing. Perhaps I should get my ears . . . syringed.

> *She sits in the armchair.*

Edwin How was your day?

Dorothy Oh, well – you know. Oh, my apron – sorry!

> *She scuttles off to the kitchen, and returns without the apron.*

Victoria's doing her homework.

She closes the door and sits in the armchair.

I've had the most frightful headache.

Edwin Have you?

Dorothy Yes, it lasted all day.

Edwin Oh, dear.

Dorothy It's a bit better now.

Edwin Did you take anything?

Dorothy Yes, I took two Disprins, but I'm afraid I gave in to it, and went to bed for a couple of hours this afternoon.

Edwin Oh, well done.

Dorothy Oh – the new girl started today.

Edwin Of course. Was she satisfactory?

Dorothy Yes . . . well, er – yes. Touch wood.

Edwin Splendid.

Dorothy Oh! Guess what?

Edwin What?

Dorothy She's from Donegal.

Edwin Really?

Dorothy Yes, I told her about Nanny.

Edwin Did you?

Dorothy Yes.

Edwin Dear old Willie.

Dorothy Yes.

    Pause.

Edwin What a coincidence.

Dorothy Indeed.

Pause.

Edwin My knee was playing up again today.

Dorothy Oh, bad luck.

Edwin Yes. Just a twinge, you know.

Dorothy Yes. Yes, horrible. Still, not long now.

Edwin No, indeed.

Dorothy Soon you'll be able to put that old desk behind you for ever.

Edwin I couldn't get a seat again this evening.

Dorothy Oh!

Edwin Yes. I had to stand as far as Richmond.

Dorothy Oh, Edwin. Did nobody get up for you?

Edwin No.

Dorothy Dreadful manners.

Edwin It was different before the war.

Dorothy Everything was different before the war.

Edwin It's just a stab – you know. And then it's gone.

Dorothy Perhaps it's arthritis.

Edwin Oh, I do hope not.

Dorothy You don't suppose arthritis is hereditary, do you?

Edwin I really couldn't say.

Dorothy I don't think it ever afflicted Mother.

Edwin No, nor Father.

Dorothy No.

Edwin Well, there's nothing to worry about then.

He lights his pipe. Dorothy gets up, takes out a cigarette and lights it. She wanders over to her husband's photograph, and looks at it. She begins to hum the tune of 'Goodnight, Sweetheart' by Noble, Campbell and Connelly. She sits in the armchair. Edwin goes over to the sideboard, and pours a sherry each for Dorothy and himself. Dorothy now begins to sing the actual words of the song, picking up where her humming left off. Edwin gives her the sherry and returns to the sofa. He joins in with her singing, harmonising with her. They both have good singing voices and sing beautifully.

Dorothy (*singing*)
Tears and parting –

Dorothy *and* **Edwin** (*singing*)
May make us forlorn
But, with the dawn,
A new day is born.

Goodnight, sweetheart,
Though I'm not beside you,
Goodnight, sweetheart,
Still my love will guide you.
Dreams enfold you –
In each one I'll hold you.
Goodnight, sweetheart, goodnight.

Edwin Chin-chin!

Dorothy Chin-chin!

They sip their sherry. Victoria opens the door and enters.

Victoria When's dinner?

Dorothy Oh – goodness me!

She gets up and scuttles towards the door.

Victoria Have you forgotten?

Dorothy No, darling. Of course I haven't forgotten.

She scuttles back to put down her sherry glass.

Victoria What are we having?

Dorothy Meatballs, with boiled potatoes and cabbage.

Victoria I hate meatballs.

Dorothy Yes, I know you do, darling.

Dorothy exits to the kitchen.

Victoria (*after her*) When will it be ready?

Dorothy (*off*) About half an hour, I should think.

Pause. Victoria comes into the room a little.

Victoria Hello, Uncle Edwin.

Edwin Hello. And how was Victoria's day?

Victoria It was okay, I s'pose.

Edwin Oh, it was 'okay', was it?

Victoria Yes. It was okay.

Edwin Good. Good.

Victoria exits, closing the door behind her. Edwin sips his sherry.
Fade lights.

SCENE FOUR

A Saturday afternoon in November.
  Lights up. Hugh enters briskly, talking as he goes.
*Edwin follows him, carrying a tray of tea things. During
the following, Hugh sets a side table in front of the sofa
and Edwin puts down the tray. Hugh sits on the sofa.
Edwin closes the door, then joins Hugh.*

Hugh We're terribly proud of Geoffrey, you know.

Edwin I'm sure you are.

Hugh He's doing phenomenally well up in Manchester.

Edwin Yes.

Hugh He's a very industrious chap. I don't know where
he gets that from. He's letting down the family tradition
of mediocrity. He's got his MSc and now he's working
with Ferranti.

Edwin shuts the door and joins Hugh on the sofa.

Edwin They make television sets, don't they?

Hugh They also make computers, whatever they may be.
I said to him, 'Geoffrey, what exactly is a computer?'
And his explanation lasted all the way through lunch and
dinner, and I still didn't understand a word of it.

Edwin It's all very baffling, isn't it?

Hugh Very baffling. He's a research fellow now, you
know. I said to him, 'You're a man of the future – I'm a
man of the past.' (*Laughs.*) We're yesterday's men.

Edwin Indeed.

Hugh Shall I be mother?

Edwin Oh, thank you.

Hugh pours the tea.

Hugh Now Edwin, I'm going to tell you something in the strictest confidence, and it's something I wouldn't tell anyone else.

Edwin Oh, dear.

Hugh (*solemnly*) It's a matter of the utmost gravity, and it concerns my good lady wife. Who is, of course, a woman of unimpeachable dignity.

He finishes pouring the tea.

Now Edwin, the fact is, that Ethel . . . snores!

Hugh laughs uproariously.

It's not a serious condition, but it is an incurable one. And it accounts for the fact that I didn't sleep very well last night.

Edwin I'm sorry to hear that.

Hugh She's like a little pig. (*Snoring sound.*) Three a.m., I'm lying there. 'To pee or not to pee. That is the question!'

Edwin Yes, that is the question.

They laugh.

Hugh No, Ethel and I have now reached a momentous decision, actually.

Edwin Oh?

Hugh We've always prided ourselves on our spirit of adventure, don't you know.

Edwin Yes.

Hugh And so, we've decided not to take our holidays in the Tyrol any more.

Edwin Ah, you did say last year you thought it was getting a bit much.

Hugh Yes. The mountains have become rather steep, and so we've chosen somewhere flat, in principle.

Edwin Where would that be?

Hugh North Norfolk.

Edwin Oh, that was dear Victor's part of the world.

He looks round at Dorothy's husband's photograph.

Cromer, very nice.

Hugh (*looking at photograph briefly*) Oh yes – Victor. Poor fellow. Tragic.

Edwin Yes.

Pause. They drink their tea.

Hugh What do you make of this dog in the Sputnik, what's-its-name –

Edwin Laika.

Hugh (*overlapping*) Laika.

Edwin Oh, I don't know. I think it's a good thing. Progress has to be made.

Hugh Well, they couldn't send a man up there.

Edwin Indeed.

Hugh I think they should have sent a monkey. (*Laughs.*)

Edwin Oh, you've never got on with monkeys, have you?

Hugh No, I have not!

Pause. Suddenly, Hugh leaps at Edwin doing a loud monkey impersonation. Edwin responds similarly. They laugh. Pause.

Edwin Your sister never took us to Regent's Park again! (*Pause.*) How is she, Alice?

Hugh A bit lonely. Four grandchildren. Soldiering on.

Pause.

Edwin I've been getting that pain in my knee again.

Hugh Oh, have you?

Edwin Yes, just a stab – you know. And then it's gone.

Hugh Have you seen your chap about it? What's-his-name?

Edwin No, no – I haven't bothered.

Hugh Perhaps you should.

Edwin What do you think he'd say?

Hugh Well, I know what I'd say.

Edwin What?

Hugh Old age. Anno Domini, old bean. Nothing you can do about it. 'Where there's death, there's hope!' (*Laughs.*)

Pause.

Now, how about your retirement? I expect you're looking forward to that, aren't you, old chap?

Edwin Oh, well . . . You know.

Hugh Eh?

Edwin (*pause*) It's been forty-five years.

Hugh Any regrets?

Edwin No, no.

Hugh Good, good.

Edwin I shall probably miss the chaps.

Hugh I expect they'll give you a party, won't they?

Edwin No, only a presentation.

Hugh Gold watch?

Edwin We get a silver salver. Engraved.

Hugh Oh, I say.

Edwin I'm afraid I shall have to mutter a few words.

Hugh Jolly good! All's well that ends. (*Laughs.*) D'you know, I can't imagine retiring. I don't know what I'd do with myself all day.

Edwin Don't you chaps have to retire at some point?

Hugh I suppose I could get struck off. Depends how many more patients I manage to kill. (*Laughs.*) Very nasty, this Asian flu business, you know.

Edwin It's kept you pretty busy, I imagine?

Hugh It has, it has. Mostly home visits. Couldn't get them out of bed, poor blighters.

Edwin Any fatalities?

Hugh Oh, three or four.

Edwin Oh, dear.

Hugh No, no – you'll be fine with your books and your bloody pipe. You'll be like a dog with two tails. D'you know, I've never really understood what it is you do. I mean, what exactly is 'engrossing'?

Edwin It's writing documents.

Hugh And is it engrossing?

Edwin No, not really.

Hugh laughs.

Hugh Have you had your letter about the Old Boys' reunion in January?

Edwin Oh, very likely.

Hugh D'you think you might come this time?

Edwin Oh – no, no.

Hugh Oh, go on!

Edwin No, no – I don't think so.

Hugh Snotty'll be there. Percy Hooper. Lacey.

Edwin Will the dreaded Budleigh-Clarke be in charge again?

Hugh Oh, yes. He'll be presiding over the proceedings. Pontificating pompously, as though he were sentencing at the Old Bailey.

Edwin Bully.

Hugh It'll be a very jolly evening. Excellent beef. Do come!

Edwin No, thank you.

Hugh Oh well, I shan't ask you again. As I've said before, I never repeat myself. (*Laughs.*) Game of cards?

Edwin Oh, splendid – yes.

Hugh now moves some furniture so that Edwin can set up a folding card table.

Hugh Is it really forty years? Incredible.

Edwin Forty-five, as a matter of fact. 1913. Straight from school.

Hugh Of course.

He takes a pack of cards and a notebook and pencil from a drawer in the sideboard.

I was saying to Ethel at breakfast only this morning, that dreadful Spanish flu, end of the first war, just as I was being demobbed. When we thought we'd packed up our troubles in our old kit bags and smile, smile, smile, not a bit of it.

They put on their reading glasses.

Edwin It afflicted thousands of chaps in the trenches too, didn't it?

Hugh It did, it did. It didn't abate till the middle of 1920.

He unpacks the cards.

Geoffrey got a First, you know, with honours.

Edwin Yes, I know, you've told me. Many times.

Hugh Oh, have I?

Edwin And you went up for his graduation.

Hugh Yes, we did, and very proud parents we were. Ethel wept. (*Laughs.*)

Edwin collects their teas and brings them to the card table.

First time I've been to Manchester, and the last, I hope. Geoffrey loves it.

Edwin 'Amongst these dark, satanic mills.'

Hugh Indeed.

He shuffles the cards.

Would you care to cut the cards, old boy?

Edwin cuts them, and scores higher than Hugh.

Edwin Mine.

He proceeds to deal the cards.

Hugh Awful, dirty place. It rained cats and dogs. We did manage a few days up in Windermere, though. Very good walking country, and we were lucky with the weather.

He examines his cards.

Fee, fi, fo, fum . . . Ubi pus, ubi evacua . . . 'Twas brillig, and the slithy toves . . .

Dorothy and Victoria enter the house; the front door slams. The following dialogues overlap until Dorothy enters the room:

Hugh (*hearing the door*) Oh, I expect that's your delightful sister.

Hugh knocks on the table to start the game, but Edwin pauses. The following overlaps with Dorothy and Victoria's dialogue in the hall.

Edwin Oh, I think . . . em . . .

Hugh Oh, yes. Yes of course, old chap. We shouldn't want to, er . . .

Edwin No.

> **Dorothy** (*off*) Oh, please don't slam the door.
>
> **Victoria** (*off*) I didn't slam the door.
>
> **Dorothy** (*off*) Yes, you did.
>
> **Victoria** (*off*) I did not.
>
> **Dorothy** (*off*) Would you like me to make you a sandwich?
>
> **Victoria** (*off*) No.
>
> *She goes upstairs.*
>
> **Dorothy** (*off*) 'No, *thank you*', Victoria! You must be starving.

Victoria (*off*) Well, I'm not.

Dorothy (*off*) Well, I'm going to make some tea. Why don't you have some cake.

> *No reply. Dorothy enters the room. She is wearing her hat and coat. She speaks to Victoria as she enters.*

Dorothy 'Yes please' or 'no, thank you', Victoria! Honestly! Oh – goodness me! Hello, Hugh!

Hugh (*getting up*) Hello, Dorothy. How nice to see you.

Dorothy I'm sorry . . .

Hugh Oh, no, no.

Dorothy Well, this is a pleasant surprise. How nice to see you.

Hugh Thank you.

Dorothy Oh, I see you've been playing a spot of . . . How lovely.

Hugh Yes, we've just finished our game, haven't we?

Edwin Yes.

Hugh All's well that ends! (*Laughs.*) Very enjoyable.

Edwin Indeed.

Dorothy That's nice, Edwin. You've had a bit of company.

Edwin Yes. I'm afraid I was unable to persuade Hugh to take a biscuit.

Hugh No – it's nil by mouth for me today, I'm afraid.

Dorothy Oh, you might have offered him the sponge.

> *Hugh laughs uproariously.*

Oh – I'll just take my hat and coat off. How's Ethel?

Hugh Oh, she's hale and hearty, you know. Sleeps like a log.

Dorothy Oh, jolly good.

Hugh Yes, I was just telling Edwin about Geoffrey. We're terribly proud of him, you know. We hardly ever see him, of course. He's a research fellow now, you know – Manchester University. He's with Ferranti. Computers, whatever they are. I can't understand them, myself. It makes me feel terribly old-fashioned when he talks about them. But he's a very industrious chap – he works like a black, you know. We're terribly proud of him.

Dorothy Would you excuse me just one moment?

Hugh Yes, of course.

Dorothy goes out to remove her hat and coat.

Shall I put the cards away?

Edwin Oh, thank you. We didn't get very far this time, did we?

Hugh Just as well for you. I was going to win. (*Laughs.*)

Edwin returns the teacups to the tray. Dorothy returns.

Dorothy Oh, let me do that, Edwin.

She picks up the tea tray. Hugh puts back the furniture. Edwin proceeds to fold up the card table.

Hugh Now, we'll just put your house back in order. The animals went in two by two . . . The elephant and the kangaroo . . .

Dorothy Oh, thank you, Hugh.

Hugh Edwin tells me you've been on a shopping expedition.

Dorothy Oh, yes.

Hugh Up to town?

Dorothy Kensington High Street, actually.

Hugh I trust it was productive.

Dorothy Not particularly, no.

Hugh Oh, bad luck.

Edwin Didn't you find it?

Dorothy No, I'm afraid we didn't.

Hugh Were you looking for anything in particular?

Dorothy A winter coat for Victoria.

Edwin puts back the card table by the sideboard.

Hugh Oh, how is Victoria, by the way?

Dorothy Oh, yes, she's splendid, thank you, Hugh. Swotting like mad for her mocks, you know.

Hugh Oh, jolly good!

Dorothy takes the tea tray to the kitchen.

Well, I think perhaps I should be making tracks.

Edwin Oh, must you, old horse? You've only just arrived.

Hugh picks up Edwin's pipe.

Hugh Are you still puffing away at this thing?

Edwin Oh, yes.

Hugh You shouldn't, you know. It'll kill you.

Edwin Will it?

Hugh Yes. But never mind: I'll have a drink at your funeral. All's well that ends. (*Laughs and puts down the* *pipe.*) Now, look here, old chap. It's high time you came over to see us, you know. Ethel'll rustle you up a bit of supper.

Edwin Oh, thank you.

Enter Dorothy, who has been upstairs.

Dorothy She's just coming.

Hugh Jolly good. Geoffrey was a great all-rounder, you know. Ten 'O'-levels, flying colours. We were immensely proud of him.

Dorothy Yes, I'm sure.

Hugh We all thought he might flunk Scripture, but no – he sailed through it, like a camel in the desert.

Dorothy Gosh.

She goes to the bottom of the stairs.

Victoria.

Victoria is coming down the stairs. Dorothy returns to the room.

Here she comes.

Hugh He had a place at Cambridge, you know.

Victoria stands in the doorway.

Hello, young lady.

Victoria Hello, Dr Fennimore.

Dorothy Come in, darling.

Victoria does so, a little.

Hugh How are you?

Victoria I'm very well, thank you. How are you?

Hugh I'm very well, thank you. What have you been doing? Have you been reading a book?

Victoria Yes.

Hugh Do you read lots of books?

Victoria Yes.

Hugh Do you read them for pleasure, or for school work, or both?

Victoria Both.

Hugh Mother tells me you've been swotting for your mock turtle soups.

He laughs uproariously. Edwin laughs. Dorothy smiles. Victoria doesn't.

I expect *you're* a bit of an all-rounder, aren't you? Pretty good at everything, eh?

Victoria –

Pause.

Hugh And you've been on a shopping spree.

Victoria Yes.

Hugh Were you looking for anything in particular?

Dorothy No.

Victoria Yes. A duffle coat.

Hugh Oh, jolly good.

Victoria But Mummy won't let me have one.

Hugh Oh, dear.

Dorothy That's not quite true, darling.

Victoria Yes it is.

Dorothy No, I'm afraid it isn't.

Victoria You know it is. (*To Hugh.*) I think they're very warm and practical and fashionable, and all the girls in my class have one except for me.

Dorothy The problem with them, Hugh, is that they're not waterproof.

Victoria (*to Dorothy*) They have a hood.

Dorothy (*to Hugh*) And the gaps between the buttons at the front let the wind in.

Victoria They're not buttons, Mummy – they're toggles.

Dorothy Toggles – toggles, yes . . .

Victoria Why can't you call them toggles? That's what they are.

Dorothy Please, let's not discuss this now.

Victoria You never want to discuss anything. Ever.

Hugh Terribly modern, aren't they, these duffle coats? Very 'with it'.

Victoria You see, Mummy: Dr Fennimore likes them.

Hugh Oh, no, I didn't say that, Victoria.

Dorothy Well, perhaps we'll have another jaunt next weekend.

Victoria Why, are you going to change your mind? Lovely to see you again, Dr Fennimore.

Hugh Very nice to see you, too, Victoria. Don't work too hard.

    Victoria goes upstairs. Pause.

Well, I think perhaps I should be wending my weary way.

Dorothy Oh, that's a shame, Hugh.

Hugh Very nice to see you, Dorothy.

Dorothy Yes. Please do give my very best to Ethel.

Hugh Of course. If the weather's fine we're rather hoping to get in a bracing walk at Box Hill tomorrow.

Dorothy Oh, lovely.

Hugh Goodbye, Dorothy.

Dorothy Goodbye, Hugh.

Edwin and Hugh go into the hall.

Edwin (*off*) Did you have a hat?

Hugh (*off*) I did, and here it is. Will I see you at church tomorrow?

Edwin opens the front door.

Edwin (*off*) Of course.

Hugh (*off*) Cheerio.

Edwin (*off*) Goodbye, old chap.

The front door closes. Edwin comes back into the room, and sits on the sofa.

Dorothy I think I'll lie down for half an hour before sherry.

Edwin Very well.

Dorothy exits, closing the door behind her. Pause. Fade lights.

SCENE FIVE

A November weekday afternoon.

Victoria is lying on the sofa, smoking a cigarette. A couple of popular film annuals, her shoes and her satchel are strewn on the floor around her. A half-full bottle of Coca-Cola and a chocolate bar are on the side table.

Dorothy is heard at the front door. Victoria quickly puts out the cigarette in an ashtray, puts the drink on the floor, and hides the chocolate in her satchel. She is standing as Dorothy enters. Dorothy has her hat and coat on, and is holding a bunch of flowers.

Victoria Hello, Mummy.

Dorothy Hello, darling! What are you doing home?

Victoria They're very beautiful flowers.

Dorothy Why aren't you at school?

Victoria I have a terrible headache and I've come home early.

She sits on the sofa.

Dorothy Oh, dear. Have you taken anything?

Victoria Yes, I have.

Dorothy moves further into the room. She puts down her handbag.

Dorothy What did you take?

Victoria Some aspirin.

Dorothy Why didn't you take Disprin?

Victoria I meant Disprin.

Pause.

Dorothy Victoria, have you been smoking?

Victoria No, of course not.

Dorothy Don't be absurd!

Victoria I haven't even smoked all of it.

Dorothy Victoria, you know how I feel about you smoking.

Victoria You smoke.

Dorothy Well, that's beside the point. I'm an adult. And you've been drinking that ghastly Coca-Cola.

Victoria Oh, please stop being so boring, Mummy.

Pause.

Dorothy I'm just going to put these in some water.

She proceeds out of the room, but stops in the doorway.

Victoria, do you really have a headache?

Victoria (*standing up*) Yes, of course I have a headache, I'm not lying.

Dorothy I'm not suggesting that you are lying.

Victoria Yes, you are.

Dorothy No, I'm not.

Victoria You're calling me a liar.

Dorothy I'm merely trying to ascertain whether you do indeed have a headache . . . or whether you've been playing truant.

Victoria How dare you accuse me of truanting? I have a terrible headache, and I came home early, and you weren't even here to look after me, and I've had to be on my own all afternoon.

Dorothy Yes, I'm sorry I wasn't here when you got back. I went up to the West End.

Victoria Why are you saying vile things to me? You're being horrible.

Dorothy No, I'm not, darling.

Victoria You're being completely unfair.

Dorothy Please, Victoria – please, I've never done anything other than look after you and love you.

Victoria Oh, stop it.

Dorothy Why are you so angry with me all the time? You used to be such a well-behaved little girl during the war. Your daddy would have been so proud of you.

Victoria Oh, don't bring Daddy into it! I never even knew him.

Dorothy I only ever try to do my best.

Victoria collects her things.

Victoria I hate you!

She goes upstairs and slams her bedroom door.
Dorothy goes to the kitchen with the flowers. Pause. She returns. She is still wearing her hat and coat, but she is empty-handed. She picks up the vase of flowers on the sideboard and takes them out to the kitchen.
Fade lights.

SCENE SIX

A little later: evening.
Enter Edwin. He goes to the sideboard, and pours two sherries. Enter Dorothy, carrying the vase, in which are the new flowers. She puts it on the sideboard. Then she

proceeds to close the curtains. Edwin begins to sing. She joins him: 'Smile', by John Turner and Geoffrey Parsons.

Edwin (*singing*)
   Smile, though your heart is aching –

Edwin *and* **Dorothy** (*singing*)
   Smile, even though it's breaking.
   When there are clouds in the sky, you'll get by.
   If you smile, through your tears and sorrow,
   Smile, and maybe tomorrow
   You'll see the sun come shining through,
   If you just smile.

Pause. Edwin gives Dorothy her sherry.

Edwin Chin-chin.

Dorothy Chin-chin.

Pause. They sip their sherry.
   Fade lights.

SCENE SEVEN

Early December. A weekday afternoon.
   Gertrude and Muriel are sitting on the sofa, looking at a woman's magazine. Both are wearing reading glasses. Gertrude has on her hat. She turns a page. Something amuses them, and they both roar with laughter. Then Gertrude changes the subject.

Gertrude How d'you think she's looking?

Muriel Well, quite frankly, Gertrude –

Gertrude She seems terribly tired.

Muriel Yes.

Gertrude Very pale.

31

Muriel Yes, and a little grey.

Gertrude I mean, she's never slept well, has she?

Muriel Never.

Gertrude It's the perennial problem.

Muriel Yes.

Gertrude Very sad.

Muriel Yes.

Gertrude Now, you know what she's like.

Muriel Yes.

Gertrude If we approach this too directly, she's likely to turn round and do the opposite thing.

Muriel Yes.

Gertrude I love her to bits, but she can be frightfully stubborn.

Muriel Yes.

Gertrude So, mum's the word.

Muriel Yes.

Gertrude Sun, sea and sand!

Muriel Quite.

Gertrude My dear, you're looking absolutely lovely.

Muriel Oh, thank you, Gertrude.

Gertrude It's so nice to see you. I must just go and hang up my hat.

She gets up, and proceeds towards the door.

Now, Dorothy . . .

Dorothy enters with a tea trolley. She is wearing her apron.

Oh, there you are! Wonderful! I'm gasping for a cup of tea.

Dorothy Good. So am I!

Gertrude disappears into the hall. Muriel has put the magazine away, and goes to Dorothy.

Muriel Now, let me help.

Dorothy Oh, would you, Muriel? Thank you.

Muriel begins taking plates from the trolley, but then helps Dorothy to move a chair.

Muriel Oh, no . . .

Dorothy Thank you.

Gertrude returns. Dorothy moves a side table, and Muriel sets out the plates.

Gertrude Good. Oh, Dorothy – what a dear little pinny!

Dorothy Oh, sorry . . . Here are the napkins, Muriel.

Muriel Thank you, darling.

Dorothy I'll just run and take it off.

She scuttles off to the kitchen.

Gertrude Oh dear, she's quite incorrigible. It's only us. She has no need to stand on ceremony.

Gertrude and Muriel sit down.

My dear! That is such a sweet little outfit. That turquoise enhances the sparkle in your eyes.

Muriel Oh, you are kind.

Dorothy returns and picks up a plateful of sandwiches.

Gertrude Dorothy, I'm just telling Muriel what a charming ensemble she's wearing. She always did have impeccably good taste.

Dorothy Oh, yes.

Gertrude Darling – do stand up and show me the full effect.

Muriel Oh, don't be silly.

Gertrude Come along! Give me a twirl. I insist!

Muriel I'm too old to twirl.

Gertrude stands.

Gertrude Up you get! On the catwalk!

Muriel gets up, reluctantly. Dorothy joins them to watch, holding the plate of sandwiches.

Muriel (*twirling*) 'As modelled by Mrs Muriel Underwood . . .'

Gertrude That is a beautifully cut suit.

Muriel Thank you.

Dorothy And hemlines are getting shorter, aren't they?

Gertrude Oh, yes.

Muriel You don't think it's a little long?

Dorothy No.

Gertrude No, that length is terribly flattering to the ankle.

Muriel Oh, because I shouldn't want to look old-fashioned.

Gertrude You don't at all, my dear. Quite up-to-the-minute.

She examines Muriel's scarf.

34

Is this Hermès?

Muriel (*amused*) No! I bought it in Richmond, actually.

Gertrude Richmond! Oh, you're such a clever girl. There am I, chasing all over the West End for the perfect accessory, and you find this delightful little item in Richmond. I'm very jealous. Oh, thank you, Dorothy – I'm absolutely famished.

She takes a sandwich.

Dorothy Oh, dear!

Gertrude sits down and takes a bite of sandwich. Muriel sits, too. Dorothy offers her the sandwiches.

Muriel?

Muriel (*taking one*) Ooh, delicious.

Dorothy Sorry, they're only cucumber.

Muriel Oh, don't be silly.

Dorothy returns the sandwiches to the trolley and sets about pouring the teas.

Gertrude Now, I want to hear all your news. How is my beloved godson? How is Bernard?

Muriel He's doing terribly well, thank you.

Gertrude I don't suppose you've heard from him recently?

Muriel Not in the last two weeks, no.

Gertrude No. It's very worrying, isn't it?

Muriel Well, it's not, if you consider –

Gertrude I mean, it's a terribly confusing situation over there, don't you think?

Muriel Yes, it is, but –

Gertrude This chap Makarios seems most peculiar.

Muriel I'd like to put him across my knee, actually.

Gertrude Oh, I say, Muriel!

Dorothy exits to kitchen.

However, I think Bernard will prove a more frequent correspondent than his big brother was when he was doing National Service.

Muriel Undoubtedly.

Gertrude And how is big brother enjoying life now that he's been demobbed?

Muriel Oh, well . . . he's certainly –

Dorothy returns with a milk jug.

Gertrude Dear Ronald! You must be so happy to have him home again!

Muriel We barely see him, actually.

Gertrude Oh, really? Why is that?

Muriel Well, he hardly ever comes home at night.

Gertrude Oh, I say! Young men these days!

Muriel Yes.

Gertrude Does he have a young lady?

Muriel Oh, no, not Ronald.

Gertrude No.

Pause. Dorothy looks at Muriel.

Well, it's the same with Adele. She's never out of the sky.

Dorothy hands Gertrude a cup of tea.

Thank you, darling. And how is my lovely goddaughter?

Dorothy Oh, well, she's –

Gertrude Not working too hard, I hope?

Dorothy No . . .

Gertrude I do sometimes worry that she does, you know.

Muriel Oh, so do I.

Gertrude And is Ronald still having an exciting time at the Grosvenor?

Muriel Well, he is working hard –

Gertrude It must be such fun being a top-notch barman, mixing all those exotic cocktails for people every night!

Muriel He's only a waiter, Gertrude.

Gertrude Oh, well – one day!

Muriel Yes.

Pause. Gertrude savours her tea.

Gertrude Oh, delicious, Dorothy. Straight from the tea-garden into the pot!

Dorothy Oh, thank you. Muriel.

She gives Muriel her tea.

Muriel Thank you, dear. Oh – I'm thinking of having Bernard's bedroom redecorated while he's in the army.

Gertrude Oh really? How lovely! Do you have any idea of colour schemes?

Muriel Not yet –

Gertrude I don't quite recall his room at present . . .

Muriel It's a sage green.

Gertrude Sage green is very masculine.

Muriel Yes, it is . . .

Gertrude So many men prefer dark colours.

Muriel Yes. But I think he ought to have something more grown-up. Before he goes to university.

Gertrude Oh yes – of course. He has a university place, doesn't he? Remind me of his subject.

Dorothy (*sitting down*) It's Chemical Engineering, isn't it?

Muriel Yes.

Gertrude Oh, yes – my! What a terribly clever boy he is!

Muriel Yes, we're very proud of him.

Gertrude And what about Victoria? Does she have any plans for her future yet?

Dorothy Oh, goodness no. She hasn't thought about it.

Gertrude No, well, it's different for a girl, isn't it? I mean, Adele at Victoria's age had absolutely no idea, and look how well things have turned out for her. My, what a terribly glamorous life she leads!

Muriel Yes.

Gertrude And is Victoria looking forward to her sixteenth birthday?

Dorothy Oh, yes – I think so . . .

Gertrude Sweet sixteen! How time flies. Tell me, is she starting to socialise a little more these days?

Dorothy Well, it's difficult, because she's –

Gertrude I do hope so. You know what they say: all work and no play . . .

Dorothy Yes.

Gertrude Does she have any friends?

Pause.

Dorothy Well, I . . .

Gertrude I mean, Adele at Victoria's age was off gallivanting at all hours. In fact, I sometimes used to wonder whether she wasn't having slightly too much fun altogether.

Muriel She took after her mother.

Gertrude Well, she took after all three of us, didn't she?

They all laugh.

Remember our misspent youth?!

Dorothy Oh, gosh.

Gertrude Oh, my – what fun we used to have!

Muriel Yes.

Gertrude Dancing two or three times a week – straight after work sometimes, didn't we?

Dorothy Gosh – I haven't danced for years.

Gertrude Oh, Dorothy, you used to do a wonderful 'black bottom'.

Dorothy Oh . . . (*Laughing.*) Yes.

Gertrude And those darling little shoes . . . 'Finale hoppers'!

Muriel Oh, yes.

Dorothy Oh, yes. I'd forgotten about those.

Gertrude We thought we were so much the 'it' thing, with our bobbed hair . . .

Muriel Shingle cuts.

Gertrude laughs.

Dorothy Oh, yes, the shingle cut. Gosh, I wouldn't mind one of those now, to tell you the truth.

Muriel Yes.

Gertrude Well, yes. They were so much easier to look after, weren't they?

Dorothy Yes.

Muriel Instead of weekly trips to the hairdresser's.

Gertrude Yes, and that awful smell of having one's hair permed.

Dorothy Oh, ghastly.

Gertrude It's the bane of my life nowadays. Oh, yes! We were such happy little flappers!

They all laugh. Pause. They sing 'Black Bottom', by Henderson, Brown and De Sylva.

Gertrude (*singing*)
Black bottom –

Gertrude *and* **Muriel** (*singing*)
A new rhythm,
When you spot 'em –

All (*singing*)
You go with 'em!
And do that black, black
Bottom all the day long!
Boo-boo-be-do, ooh!

They all laugh.

Dorothy (*getting up*) Who'd like another sandwich? Muriel?

Muriel No, thank you, dear.

Dorothy sits down again.

Gertrude Oh, my dears – now, this will make you shriek! I was reading a little article in *The Times* the other day. Apparently, something called the Sacred Congregation of . . . something or other, have in their wisdom proclaimed the Archangel Gabriel to be the patron saint of all telephonists!

They all laugh.

Dorothy Oh!

Muriel No!

Dorothy We have our own saint!

Muriel At last!

Gertrude We could have done with him back then!

Dorothy Yes, he might have protected us from Miss Waverley.

Gertrude Oh, my dear!

Muriel Don't! Dreadful woman!

Gertrude Wasn't she? That awful moustache!

Muriel Yes.

Gertrude One would have thought there was something she could do about that. Bleach it, or pluck it.

Dorothy Yes.

Muriel I know.

Gertrude (*to Muriel*) And that terrible shaking she gave you.

Muriel I thought I was going to fall off my stool.

Gertrude Although I do seem to remember you were spending rather a long time chatting to a certain distant subscriber!

Muriel (*laughing*) I was merely doing my job.

Gertrude Oh, come along, Muriel – a distant subscriber with a very charming Scottish brogue, as I recall . . .!

Muriel I don't know what you mean, Gertrude.

Gertrude Always a weakness of yours, I think.

Muriel laughs.

Dorothy Naughty Headset Seventeen!

They all laugh.

Muriel (*to Dorothy*) Oh, and – em, Headset Thirty-Seven!

Dorothy No, I was Forty-Four. Gertrude was –

Muriel Oh, Headset Forty-Four and Headset Thirty-Seven!

Gertrude *and* **Dorothy** Seventeen, Thirty-Seven and Forty-Four!

Pause. They reflect.

Dorothy Ah!

Gertrude 'Are you there, distant subscriber?'

They all laugh.

Dorothy 'Putting you through now.'

Muriel 'Number, please.'

All No, no – 'Rubber knees!'

Gertrude 'I am terribly sorry, subscriber – your time is up.'

Dorothy Colonel!

They all laugh.

Gertrude Yes! The Colonel! My word.

Pause.

Dorothy (*getting up*) Would you like some cake, ladies?

Gertrude Might I be frightfully naughty and ask you for a cigarette?

Dorothy Oh, yes – of course.

Muriel May I, too?

Dorothy Yes. I think I'll join you.

She hands round the cigarettes.

Muriel Thank you.

Gertrude Thank you, my darling. Oh! My dears – Adele received yet another bouquet of red roses last week. Absolutely enormous. It practically filled my entire hall, and, as we know, I do not have a small hall.

Muriel Who was it from?

Gertrude Well, I only wish I knew. She very carefully removed the gift tag, leaving poor Mummy in the dark, as usual. I've really no idea why she never confides in me. Oh, she's such a wicked girl, but I do adore her. Oh – and you'll never guess who she had on board her flight at the weekend. Well, you won't guess, so I'll tell you. Pearl Carr and Teddy Johnson.

Dorothy Oh, how lovely.

Muriel Oh, gosh.

Gertrude She's terribly pretty, apparently. Lovely complexion. Oh – and her friend, Jenny, had, on her Bermuda flight the other week, Bob Hope.

Dorothy No!

Muriel Oh!

Gertrude Very quiet man, apparently. Not the least bit funny. But of course they're trained to treat these people just like any other passenger, and carry on as per normal.

Muriel I couldn't do it.

Dorothy No, I don't think I could, either.

Muriel I just couldn't.

Gertrude Nor me, frankly. Of course, she's staying at the Lexington Hotel again this week, so she'll be having all sorts of fun in the Hawaiian Room, which is her favourite Manhattan club. She is rather fond of the Park Sheraton, of course, which is terribly smart, Eleanor Roosevelt stayed there. Now: apparently, in the middle of August, there was a mobster killing on the seventeenth floor.

Dorothy Oh, gosh!

Gertrude The bathroom was riddled with bullets.

Muriel Oh!

Gertrude My! What an exciting life she leads! Lucky girl. She takes it all in her stride. I'm very proud of her.

Pause. Then Muriel coughs ostentatiously, and catches Gertrude's eye.

Gertrude Oh yes – of course. So, Muriel, what are your summer holiday plans for next year? Will you be returning to the Côte d'Azur?

Muriel Oh, yes, but this time we're going to try Cap Ferrat.

Gertrude Oh, how lovely. Well, of course, we shall be revisiting Cannes ourselves. Cedric absolutely adores it.

He's more than happy just sitting on the terrace at the Carlton Hotel, drooling over the continental cars gliding up and down the Croisette. Whilst I concentrate on my glass of champagne. So: what about you, Dorothy? What are your holiday plans?

Dorothy Oh, goodness me, we haven't even thought about it yet.

Gertrude Well, I think you should. You can never start planning too early, can you Muriel?

Muriel No, which is why –

Gertrude I think you should nudge that big brother of yours into trying somewhere somewhat further afield than, shall we say, Sidmouth.

Muriel Yes.

Dorothy Yes, we've never been abroad.

Gertrude No, you haven't. This is exactly my point. It would do you so much good. Sun, sea and sand.

Muriel Yes, and you wouldn't have to go anywhere too hot to begin with. You could try Normandy, or Brittany.

Gertrude Absolutely.

Dorothy Yes, well, I did suggest going to France . . . years ago, now.

Gertrude Well, I think you should insist. They're all the same, you know – they do tend to get stuck in a rut. If it weren't for me, Cedric and I should still be spending every summer at the dreary old Grand Hotel in Brighton. I'm sure Gerald's the same. You'd both be languishing at the Imperial, Torquay.

Muriel Precisely. We don't want to go there again.

Gertrude One does have to be rather firm, you know.

Muriel Yes.

Dorothy Well, it's not quite the same for me, is it?

Gertrude Why ever not?

Dorothy Well, you know. (*Pause.*) And as a matter of fact, I have rather fond memories of the Grand Hotel in Brighton. (*Pause.*) Because it's where Victor and I spent our honeymoon.

Muriel Oh . . .

Gertrude Oh – yes, of course, my darling. I wasn't thinking.

Muriel No.

Gertrude Silly girl. But then I always was a dreadful chatterbox, wasn't I? 'Garrulous Gertie'.

Muriel (*laughing*) Yes.

> *Pause.*

Dorothy It doesn't matter. (*Getting up.*) Let's have some more tea.

Muriel Oh, yes please.

Gertrude Oh, yes; just an inch for me, thank you.

Dorothy Yes. (*Handing Muriel a tea.*) Muriel, darling.

Muriel Thank you.

Gertrude (*getting up*) Now, do excuse me, my dears: I'm just going to pop upstairs and powder my nose. I shan't be a moment. Oh, now, my dear – how is your new little woman getting on?

Muriel Oh, yes – how is she?

Dorothy Oh, yes – well, she's . . .

Gertrude I must say, it's all looking absolutely spotless.

Sets off through the doorway, and turns back.

Oh, now, before I forget. I seem to have been nominated yet again to chair another fundraising committee.

Muriel Oh, have you?

Gertrude Yes. Call me 'Muggins'. This time, my ladies are raising money for a garden at the Cottage Hospital, which will incorporate a bench and a stone plaque, inscribed with thanks to the local Rotarians for their great philanthropic efforts. Now, we need to raise one thousand pounds by March the first, which should not be beyond the wit of man. I mean, after all, in 1944 we managed to raise seven hundred and two thousand pounds for the war effort, during 'Salute the Soldier Week' alone.

Muriel Oh, yes.

Gertrude Now, my dear Muriel, I was rather hoping that I might call upon your services yet again in your capacity as my Clothes-Collector-in-Chief.

Muriel Oh, yes, of course.

Gertrude Oh, that's marvellous! Thank you so much! And Dorothy – any small items you might have in your wardrobe would be most gratefully received.

Dorothy Oh, yes – I'll have a look.

Gertrude One doesn't want to be a snob about these things, but it does help to collect from ladies of a certain class. It rather avoids the moth problem.

Muriel She won't find a moth in sight, will she, Dorothy?

Dorothy I hope not.

Gertrude Now – my Christmas party. I'm afraid I have just had a slight contretemps with the printer, silly man. But, he assures me that the invitations will be with me by tomorrow lunchtime. However, I do expect both of you to be there in any case, as usual, on the Saturday before Christmas.

Muriel We wouldn't dream of missing it.

Gertrude Wonderful! Well, I shall pop your invitations in the post ASAP.

Muriel Take it as read – we accept.

Dorothy Yes.

Gertrude goes into the hall. At this moment, Victoria enters at the front door.

Gertrude (*off*) Oh, I say! Hello, my dear!

She comes back into the room. Dorothy gets up.

Somebody's arrived.

Muriel (*leaping up, and going to the door of the room*) Oh, who can it be?

Gertrude Here she comes.

Victoria enters.

Muriel Oh, Victoria, my darling girl. How lovely to see you! What a surprise!

Dorothy Hello, darling.

Victoria Hello, Mummy. Hello, Auntie Gertrude. Hello, Auntie Muriel.

Gertrude Have you had an exhausting day at school?

Dorothy Would you like some tea and cake?

Muriel Oh, do join us.

Gertrude Yes – Mummy's bought some delicious gateau, and we haven't even touched it yet.

Victoria Yes, some tea would be lovely, thank you.

Dorothy Yes, I'll just get another cup and saucer – excuse me.

Dorothy goes to the kitchen. Victoria goes into the hall to remove her hat and coat. Muriel follows her to the doorway.

Gertrude Oh, dear – I must dash.

She goes upstairs.

Muriel (*to Victoria*) D'you know, I do believe you've grown! Come along – come and sit with us.

She guides Victoria to the sofa. Dorothy returns and pours some tea for Victoria.

Now, how is my beautiful goddaughter? I haven't seen you for ages. Are you working terribly hard? You must be.

Dorothy Yes, she has her mock examinations after Christmas.

Muriel Oh, of course – the dreaded mocks. I remember them only too well. We had to bully Ronald, whereas Bernard you could leave to his own devices – my little genius!

Dorothy gives Victoria her tea, and passes Muriel's tea to Muriel.

Dorothy Here's your tea, darling. Muriel.

Muriel Thank you, dear. Drink your tea, Victoria – it'll warm you through.

Dorothy sits in the armchair.

Dorothy Yes, it is rather chilly.

49

Muriel Yes. My goodness, you must have your head buried in books the entire time. (*To Dorothy.*) I don't know how they keep that information up there, do you?

Dorothy No, no.

Muriel (*to Victoria*) Do you have any time to socialise?

Dorothy Well . . .

Muriel (*to Dorothy*) Because she must have homework at the weekends, as well as during the week?

Dorothy Yes.

Muriel What have your subjects been today?

Victoria Latin, Scripture, Maths . . .

Muriel Is Maths still your favourite subject?

Victoria (*after a pause*) Yes.

Muriel I'm so impressed. I was terrible at Maths, weren't you, Dorothy?

Dorothy Oh yes – awful.

Muriel I still am –

Gertrude descends the stairs, and commences the following speech long before she actually enters the room.

Gertrude So, Victoria, how's my lovely goddaughter? Are you looking forward to the Christmas holidays? (*She sits.*) I'm sure you must be. What are your plans? I expect you'll be out, gallivanting with all your chums! Not spending too much of your pocket money, though, we hope?

Muriel Well, you'll need to save some for Christmas shopping, won't you?

Gertrude Oh, yes, but young girls this age don't like to save, do they? Well, Adele certainly didn't. Poor Cedric always had his hand in his pocket.

Muriel But you'll have to buy a nice present for Mummy, at least.

Gertrude Oh, yes, I think Mummy deserves a very special present, doesn't she?

Muriel And Uncle Edwin.

Gertrude Oh, yes, and Uncle Edwin, of course. Now, I've been wondering – who are your favourite pin-ups? (*Pause.*) How about James Dean? That was terribly sad, wasn't it? And what sort of music do you like? I've been reading about the Everly Brothers. They have a song called 'Wake Up, Little Susie'. Have you heard it?

Victoria Yes.

Gertrude You have! Oh good! What fun!

Muriel Bernard likes Bill Haley.

Gertrude Oh yes, but I think you'll find Bill Haley's rather passé now, Muriel. He's jolly good to dance to, though. Do you like dancing? Now! My Christmas party. I think now that you're very nearly a young lady of sixteen, would you like to come?

Muriel What a good idea!

Dorothy Oh, no, Gertrude, I don't think so.

Gertrude Oh, why not? It's no bother – I'll pop another invitation in the post. What do you think? Or are we too fuddy-duddy for you these days?

Muriel Do come – it's such fun.

Gertrude Oh yes – we do have a lovely time, don't we, Dorothy?

Dorothy Yes.

Gertrude You could help Uncle Cedric shake the cocktails.

Muriel His glamorous assistant!

Gertrude Will you come?

Victoria (*after a pause*) Yes, that would be wonderful. Thank you, Auntie Gertrude.

Gertrude Oh, marvellous – how exciting! You shall receive your very own special invitation.

She gets up. The others do likewise.

And now, my dears, I must love and leave you. My darling, thank you so much for a delightful afternoon, as always.

Dorothy Not at all.

Gertrude (*to Victoria*) Oh, look at you! Let me give you a kiss.

She kisses Victoria's cheek, leaving a lipstick mark.

Oh dear.

She wipes Victoria's cheek.

There. Are you coming now, Muriel?

Muriel Yes.

Gertrude Oh good.

She marches out to the hall, speaking as she goes.

Now, I shall ring you in the morning with details about the arrangements for the clothes collection.

Muriel (*to Victoria*) Bye-bye, my dearest girl. (*Leaving.*) I have had the most delightful afternoon, Dorothy – thank you so much.

Dorothy Jolly good.

*Dorothy sees Gertrude and Muriel out, leaving
Victoria in the room. She stops to glance at Victoria
for a moment on her way out.*

Gertrude (*off*) I do hope we didn't outstay our welcome!

Muriel (*off*) We've been having too much fun!

Gertrude (*off, laughing*) Yes.

Muriel (*off*) Bye-bye, my darling.

Dorothy (*off*) Bye-bye.

Gertrude TTFN. Be good! Bye-bye.

*Dorothy closes the front door, and comes back into
the room.*

Victoria I shan't go to the party. Just so you know.

Dorothy Well, I think it was very nice of Auntie Gertrude
to invite you.

Victoria I can't bear either of them.

*Victoria goes upstairs. We hear her bedroom door
slam. Dorothy collects up the tea things, and loads
them on to the trolley. She pauses to reflect for a
moment. Then she wheels the trolley out to the
kitchen.*
Fade lights.

SCENE EIGHT

*A weekday morning, a few days before Christmas. An
undecorated Christmas tree stands in the window.*
*Dorothy is sitting in the armchair, wearing her
spectacles, knitting. There is a knock at the door.*

Dorothy Do come in, Maureen.

Maureen enters. She is wearing her hat and coat, and she is carrying her handbag and a suitcase. She stands in the doorway.

Maureen That's me finished, Mrs Molyneux.

Dorothy Oh, jolly good.

She removes her spectacles and puts down her knitting. She takes her purse out of her handbag and goes over to Maureen.

Now, I should like to give you an extra half-a-crown this week, Christmas bonus.

Maureen That's very kind of you – thanks very much, Mrs Molyneux.

Dorothy You're welcome, Maureen. (*Searching her purse.*) Oh . . . goodness me, I'm sure I had three or four pounds in here . . . Er . . . what've I –? I must have . . .

She glances at the Christmas tree, pauses, then remembers something else.

Oh, yes . . . Gosh . . . well, you know what it's like at this time of year. Spend, spend, spend . . . I'm sorry to have to ask you this, Maureen, but were I to pay your bus fare, would you be so kind as to come back tomorrow morning, after breakfast, by which time I will have been able to go to the bank, or quite possibly borrow it from my brother?

Maureen How can I come back tomorrow morning after breakfast? Am'n't I getting the six o'clock train from Euston to Holyhead tonight, I'm getting the overnight ferry at half two in the morning from Holyhead into Dun Laoghaire. I'll be in Dublin by breakfast and I should be in Donegal by dinner time.

Dorothy I see. Perhaps I could write you a cheque?

Maureen What good's a cheque to the likes of me, Mrs Molyneux?

Dorothy Oh . . . Well, let me see, I have . . . (*Counting money.*) Three-and-fourpence-ha'penny.

Maureen Three-and-fourpence-ha'penny is a lot of good to me, and me going to do me Christmas shopping in Oxford Street before I get the train.

Dorothy Oh, I see.

Maureen Have you no way of getting the money?

Dorothy Unless you'd like to come to the bank with me now?

Maureen Sure, I'm on my way to me other job now.

Dorothy I'm so sorry, Maureen.

Maureen Give me what you have.

Dorothy Yes, of course.

She gives Maureen the money.

Maureen It's a disgrace, Mrs Molyneux – it's Christmas time, for God's sake.

Dorothy follows Maureen to the front door.

Dorothy (*off*) Yes, I am so dreadfully sorry, Maureen. Happy Christmas.

She closes the front door and comes back into the room. Pause. Then she goes to the kitchen.
    Fade lights.

Christmas Eve, evening.

The Christmas tree is half decorated. An old hatbox sits on the chair in the middle of the room.

Edwin is sitting on the sofa, smoking his pipe and reading a book. This is a Penguin paperback crime novel, and he is engrossed in the last few pages.

Dorothy enters from the kitchen. She is wearing her apron. Edwin remains engrossed in the book.

Dorothy I forgot to light the oven – silly me.

She closes the door, then takes a couple of decorations from the box and proceeds to complete the Christmas tree.

Oh, one always forgets to do behind the tree, doesn't one? It's nice for the people walking past. Brings a little warmth and cheer to their lives. Of course, Gertrude likes her tree to have a different colour theme every year, doesn't she? It was red, white and blue in Coronation year, do you remember? I didn't much care for last year's black-and-white effect. Most peculiar. Dear old Gertrude. She's having a purple tree this year. But we missed that treat, didn't we? No, I much prefer opening Mother's box each year, and greeting these dear old friends. (*She takes out a fairy.*) That's what I think a Christmas tree should be. (*To the fairy.*) Hello, little one!

Edwin glances up for a moment, but returns to his book. Dorothy continues to address the fairy.

We just need you now, don't we? To top things off. (*To Edwin.*) I'll go and get Victoria. This is her little job, isn't it?

Dorothy exits upstairs, holding the fairy. Edwin coincidentally reaches the end of his book. He closes it, and reflects on the denouement. Then he puts it down.

(*Off.*) Victoria!

Victoria (*in her room*) Yes?

Dorothy (*off*) Are you going to come and put the fairy on the tree?

She returns and stands by the tree with the fairy.

She's just coming.

Victoria enters, closing the door behind her. Edwin removes his reading glasses, replacing them with his other pair.

(*To Victoria.*) She's all ready for you.

She hands Victoria the fairy. Edwin smiles at Dorothy and crosses to the sideboard to pour some sherry.

Don't forget to make a wish.

Victoria places the fairy at the top of the tree.

There. Did you make a wish, darling?

Victoria Yes, of course.

Dorothy Good. Now Christmas can really begin. Oh – my apron. Sorry!

She scuttles off to the kitchen. Victoria joins Edwin at the sideboard.

Victoria Please may I have a sherry, Uncle Edwin?

Edwin laughs.

Why is that funny?

Dorothy returns, and shuts the door.

Dorothy Here we all are.

Victoria (*to Edwin*) Why can't I have a sherry?

Dorothy (*amused*) Oh, don't be silly!

Victoria I'm not being silly, Mummy.

   Pause.

Dorothy Of course you can't have a sherry, darling.

Victoria Why not?

Dorothy Because you're still a child.

Victoria I'm not a child.

Dorothy You're only fifteen.

Victoria I will be sixteen on the fourteenth of January.

Dorothy I've bought you some lovely pink lemonade.

Victoria I don't want any lovely pink lemonade. I'd like a sherry.

Dorothy Please, Victoria.

Victoria My birthday is only three weeks away.

Dorothy Why don't we go and get our presents and put them underneath the tree?

Victoria Uncle Edwin, would you please be so kind as to pour me a sherry?

Dorothy Victoria, when you are sixteen, you may indeed have a small sherry. But until then, I'm afraid it's out of the question. I'm sorry.

   She takes her sherry from Edwin.

Victoria You're so stupid.

Dorothy –

Victoria Why are you being so petty?

Dorothy I'm not being petty.

Victoria You are petty. You won't even let me have posters up in my room.

Dorothy That's because the Sellotape ruins the wallpaper and the paint.

Pause.

Victoria You're pathetic. Merry Christmas.

She leaves the room.

Dorothy (*as Victoria goes*) Victoria, please!

Victoria slams the door, and goes up to her bedroom, slamming that door, too. Pause.

Edwin Chin-chin.

Dorothy Chin-chin.

Pause.
  Fade lights.

SCENE TEN

Christmas Day. Late morning.
  Victoria is sitting on the sofa, reading a magazine.
A key is heard in the front door. Dorothy enters, wearing her hat and coat.

Dorothy Hello, darling.

Victoria Hello, Mummy.

Dorothy Happy Christmas.

Victoria Happy Christmas.

Dorothy goes out to hang up her coat. Edwin enters.

Edwin Merry Christmas, Victoria.

Victoria Merry Christmas, Uncle Edwin. How was church?

Edwin Very nice.

Victoria Good.

Edwin Very jolly. You were missed. Dr and Mrs Fennimore asked after you.

He goes to the sideboard to pour some sherry. Dorothy enters, shutting the door.

Dorothy What have you been up to?

Victoria Nothing.

Dorothy Have you had some breakfast?

Victoria Yes, thank you.

Dorothy Good.

Victoria Please may I have a sherry, Uncle Edwin?

Dorothy Victoria, please let's not start all this again.

Victoria I'd like a sherry.

Dorothy Victoria . . .

Victoria Mummy, it's Christmas.

Pause. Edwin carries two glasses of sherry over to the sofa, and gives one to Dorothy.

Dorothy Thank you.

Victoria Please, Uncle Edwin?

Edwin holds out the other sherry to Victoria. Pause, then Victoria takes it.

Victoria Thank you.

Dorothy Edwin, what are you doing?

Edwin doesn't reply. He returns to the sideboard.

Edwin?

Edwin turns to Dorothy, holding a third glass of sherry, which he has already poured.

Edwin It's just a short time to go. Only three weeks.

Dorothy Victoria: will you please put that glass down?

Victoria Mummy, don't make a fuss.

Dorothy Victoria, please. There are rules.

Victoria gets up, puts her sherry on the sideboard, and leaves the room. She goes upstairs. Her bedroom door closes. Dorothy looks at Edwin. She puts her sherry down. Pause. Then she goes upstairs, leaving the door open. Edwin sips his sherry and sits on the sofa.

Dorothy (*off*) Please, Victoria, it's Christmas.

Victoria (*off*) Go away.

Dorothy returns and sits down.

Edwin Is everything all right?

Dorothy No, Edwin, everything is not all right.

Edwin Is she coming down?

Dorothy She told me to go away.

Pause.

Christmas.

Edwin Just you and me. All the more turkey for us.

Dorothy gives him a sharp look.

(*Lightly.*) Let me get you another drink.

Dorothy I don't want another drink, thank you. I haven't drunk this one yet.

Edwin goes over to the sideboard and pours himself another sherry.

I have to say, Edwin, I do feel you've let me down a little.

Edwin I'm so sorry, my dear. You know I wouldn't want to hurt you. Ever.

Dorothy How do you suppose Victor would have felt if he'd known our child was drinking alcohol?

Edwin (*looking at Victor's photograph*) Well, I'm not sure. It's so close to her birthday, it's the season of good will, and somehow . . . these days . . . Well, we'll just have to try and make the best of it.

He returns to the sofa.

Dorothy I don't want to have to make the best of it. (*She gets up.*) I just want my little girl back.

She leaves, shutting the door. Edwin is left on the sofa. Pause.
Fade lights.

SCENE ELEVEN

New Year's Eve, evening.
Edwin, Dorothy and Victoria enter the room.

Edwin Very tasty!

Dorothy Thank you. I'm terribly sorry about the mint sauce.

Edwin (*laughing*) Oh, never mind.

Dorothy sits in the armchair, Edwin sits on the sofa

and Victoria picks up a woman's magazine and sits at the other end of the sofa.

Dorothy Well, I wonder what 1958 has in store for us all.

Edwin Well, I know what it holds for me.

Dorothy Yes – big change.

Edwin And a big year for Victoria.

Dorothy (*to Victoria*) Yes, darling, we shall all keep our fingers crossed for you.

Edwin Indeed.

Victoria ignores them, and reads the magazine.

Dorothy I don't expect there'll be much change for me. (*Pause.*) Why don't we get out that old card table, and play a few games?

Edwin Oh, splendid.

Dorothy Victoria?

Victoria (*without looking up*) No, thank you, Mummy.

Dorothy A spot of Ludo? Or Snakes and Ladders? Monopoly! Oh, but then we'd probably be here till next New Year's Eve!

Edwin laughs.

Oh, Victoria, you used to love staying up on New Year's Eve, in your dressing gown and bedroom slippers, eating your Smarties and your Spangles, playing Happy Families and listening to the chimes of Big Ben at midnight, didn't you?

Victoria Yes, Mummy.

She gets up and goes towards the door.

Dorothy Oh. Are you coming back, or shall we say 'Happy New Year' now?

Victoria (*turning*) Happy New Year.

Victoria leaves the room, shutting the door behind her. Long pause.

Dorothy It's funny.

Edwin What's that?

Dorothy Mother. She could never sing, could she?

Edwin (*amused*) No.

Dorothy Well, not really. But she played the piano so gracefully.

She gets up and lights a cigarette.

Do you remember New Year's Eve, 1925?

Edwin (*smiling*) I do.

Dorothy Father, in his funny hat?

Edwin Mother was furious with him. He'd passed away by Easter, poor fellow. (*Pause.*) General Strike.

Dorothy Oh, yes. He had such a lovely, mellow singing voice.

Edwin He did, he did. But he was quite dreadful on the piano.

Pause.

Dorothy Heigh-ho.

Pause. Dorothy puts out her half-smoked cigarette.

I think I shall have an early night.

Pause.

Happy New Year, Edwin.

Edwin Happy New Year, my dear.

> *Dorothy leaves, closing the door. Edwin remains on
> the sofa. Pause.*
> *Fade lights.*

SCENE TWELVE

A weekday morning.
> *Dorothy bustles in through the open door of the room.
> She bears an armful of clothes. She drapes these over the
> back of the sofa. She moves two dresses to the wooden
> chair, leaving two on the sofa. Then, hesitating a little,
> she swaps one of the garments on the sofa for one on the
> chair. She is clearly undecided about something. The
> doorbell rings. She goes out to answer it.*

Dorothy (*off*) Hello, Muriel.

Muriel (*off, stressed*) Oh, my darling Dorothy, this is
dreadful. I'm sorry I'm so late.

Dorothy Oh.

Muriel It's none of my doing, I can tell you. This wretched
weather's a nightmare. I don't know where all this traffic's
come from – you can't move.

Dorothy Yes.

> *During the above, Muriel, wearing her hat and coat,
> has rushed into the room and sat on the sofa.*

Muriel I've just driven all the way up to Canonbury and
back.

Dorothy Have you?

Muriel Yes, Gertrude will be simply thrilled. I've gathered
heaps from all corners. The ladies have been so generous.

Dorothy Oh.

Muriel Enid has put on so much weight, she's practically filled my little car with all the clothes she can't wear.

Dorothy Gosh.

Muriel How I come to have two such lumpen sisters, I do not know.

Dorothy No, and you're so trim.

Muriel Yes, I am.

Dorothy Let me make you a coffee.

She gets up. So does Muriel.

Muriel Oh, my goodness, no – I'm late, late, late. My hair appointment's at one-thirty, and I absolutely have to unload the car at home first.

Dorothy Yes, of course.

Muriel Oh, super! You've made a start. You are clever.

Dorothy Oh, well, not really.

Muriel is examining the two lots of clothes.

Muriel Dorothy, do you know? – This morning, I've had to summon up all the dignity of my sex.

Dorothy Have you?

Muriel Yes. I've been the victim of the most frightful manners.

Dorothy Gosh! What happened?

Muriel Just as I was leaving Canonbury Square, I noticed a tall man, standing at the traffic lights, looking at a map. I thought, 'Now, there's a man who's lost.' So I stopped the car in the middle of the traffic, I got out, I dashed over to him, and I said, 'Excuse me, sir, I hope you don't mind my intruding, but you appear to be lost. May I be of assistance?' Dorothy: would you believe it? He snapped at me: 'Madam, I have a tongue in my head, and if I need help, I am perfectly capable of using it. And by the way, this is not a map, and I am a representative of the Metropolitan Water Board.' And with that, he hopped on a passing bus.

Dorothy How extraordinary.

Muriel Yes. I was quite shaken.

Dorothy I'm sure you were.

Muriel So I got back into the car, and just as I was checking my face in the mirror – I was so flustered – there was a tap on the window and I thought, 'Oh no – he's back!' I turned round, and there was a terribly young bobby. So I wound down the window, feeling guilty, as you do, and he said, 'Excuse me, madam – I do hope you're going to re-adjust that mirror before you drive off.' I said, 'Of course I am, officer. I've been driving since 1943.'

Dorothy Yes, you have.

Muriel Honestly, Dorothy – you try to do good in this world.

Dorothy I know.

Muriel You know what they say: 'No good turn goes unpunished.' Now, to the job in hand. What do we have?

She puts down her handbag, and starts examining the clothes.

Dorothy Oh, yes. Well, there's this blouse.

Muriel (*inspecting it*) Good.

Dorothy I can't wear it any more, Muriel. The buttons go all the way up to the top, and it makes me feel claustrophobic.

Muriel picks up another garment.

Muriel Now, what about this?

Dorothy Well, I haven't had that very long, Muriel . . .

Muriel It's splendid.

Dorothy I've never worn it.

Muriel Oh, you are naughty.

Dorothy Yes, I don't know why I bought it in the first place.

Muriel laughs. She picks up one of the dresses lying on the sofa.

Muriel Oh, I remember this. Isn't it pretty?

Dorothy Yes, I bought it on the day I got engaged.

Muriel Oh, Dorothy.

Dorothy Yes. But look at it. I couldn't wear it now.

Muriel No. Well, it's going to make some poor little lady very happy. Thank you.

Dorothy picks up the last garment.

Dorothy I bought this dress just after the war.

Muriel Oh, it's perfect.

Dorothy But all the beading's starting to come away.

Muriel Oh, that doesn't matter – they won't notice.

She puts it on the pile of clothes.

Now, would you like me to come upstairs with you?

Dorothy Oh, what for?

Muriel To help you down with the rest.

Dorothy No – that's all I have, I'm afraid.

Muriel Oh, is it?

Dorothy Yes. I'm sorry, Muriel.

Muriel Oh well – no matter, my darling. Every little counts and you've done your best. (*Pause.*) Oh, look at me! I haven't even asked you how you are.

Dorothy Oh, I'm fine – never mind me!

She picks up the pile of clothes.

Muriel This is terrible – I'm in the most fearful rush.

Dorothy gives her the pile.

These are beautiful. Thank you! Well – onwards and upwards.

Dorothy I'm sorry, Muriel; on second thoughts, I think I might just retrieve this.

She takes the dress she bought at the time of her engagement. Muriel touches her arm.

Muriel Of course, my darling. Understood.

They proceed to the front door.

(*Off.*) I shall phone you very soon.

Dorothy (*off*) Yes, all right, Muriel.

Muriel (*off*) Thank you so much. Goodbye, my darling.

Dorothy (*off*) Bye-bye.

Dorothy closes the front door. She hovers for a moment in the doorway of the room, reflecting on her dress; then she takes it upstairs.
Fade lights.

A weekday evening in January. Victoria's birthday.
Edwin enters. He is smartly dressed, in his best suit.
He goes to the sideboard, and proceeds to pour some
sherries.
Dorothy comes down the stairs, and into the room.
She too is dressed up, as for a special occasion.

Dorothy Oh, Edwin! You look splendid.

Edwin Thank you. So do you. Charming.

Dorothy Thank you.

She joins him at the sideboard. He gives her a sherry.
She exudes an air of excited expectation.

Gosh.

Victoria enters from upstairs. She stands in the
doorway. She is wearing her school uniform. Dorothy
and Edwin are clearly shocked.

Dorothy Oh, darling, you haven't changed yet. (*Pause.*)
I thought you'd have . . . Well, never mind. Let's have our
little celebration toast and then you can pop upstairs. We
don't have to leave just yet.

Edwin offers Victoria a sherry.

Victoria No, thank you.

Dorothy It's all right darling – you can have one now.

Victoria I don't want one.

Dorothy But it's your birthday. You're sixteen.

Victoria I know.

Edwin It's your celebration drink.

Dorothy This is what you wanted.

Victoria Well, I don't want it now.

Pause.

Dorothy Well, all right. You go and get ready – the car'll be here soon.

Victoria I'm not coming.

Dorothy What do you mean, you're not coming?

Victoria I don't want to go.

Dorothy Victoria, please – it's your birthday.

Edwin We've booked the restaurant.

Victoria I don't care.

Dorothy (*touching Victoria's arm*) But this is what you said you wanted to do.

Victoria Don't touch me! I never said I wanted to do anything. You don't know what I want. You never ask me.

She runs upstairs, pursued by Dorothy.

Dorothy That's not true, darling. I only ever want to make you happy.

Victoria (*off*) Well, you don't make me happy. Leave me alone!

Victoria slams her bedroom door. We hear Dorothy crying. She goes into her bedroom, and closes the door. Edwin puts down the drinks on the sideboard. Pause. Then he goes into the kitchen, leaving the door open.
    Fade lights.

SCENE FOURTEEN

A Wednesday morning in March.

The doorbell rings. Pause. After a while, Dorothy emerges from upstairs. She is wearing a dressing gown and her earrings. She hovers in the doorway. Then she goes over to the window and peeps surreptitiously round the curtain. The doorbell rings again. Dorothy hesitates, then goes and answers the front door.

Dorothy (*off*) Hello, Gertrude . . .

Gertrude (*off*) Oh, hello, my darling! Now, fear not: I shan't be imposing on you – I can only stay for five minutes.

They enter the room.

I know it's terribly naughty of me to drop in unannounced, but I've just been rather derailed. I have a hair appointment at twelve-thirty, and I was planning to pop into Partridge's. I spent ten minutes parking the car, and when I arrived at the shop, I was confronted with a handwritten notice, telling me that they were shut, due to a bereavement. I can't imagine who could have died. I'm on the hunt for mulberry velvet for Cedric's study – you know what he's like. But, my darling – how are you?

She sits on the sofa. Dorothy joins her.

Dorothy Well, er . . .

Gertrude It's so nice to see you relaxing in a cosy housecoat!

Dorothy Oh, it's just my old dressing gown . . .

Gertrude I've not seen you since before Christmas. Well, of course, I've been completely snowed under with the committee. Oh, now: here's some fabulous news. Guess how much money we managed to raise, in the end!

Dorothy Oh – I've no idea.

Gertrude Just shy of nineteen hundred pounds!

Dorothy Gosh.

Gertrude Isn't that marvellous?

Dorothy Yes.

Gertrude It will be so nice for the poor little sick children.

Dorothy Yes. I'm so sorry, Gertrude.

Gertrude Whatever for, darling?

Dorothy I didn't have a very good night's sleep last night.

Gertrude Oh, dear.

Dorothy And I had a bad headache this morning, so I took two Disprins and went back to bed for a couple of hours.

Gertrude Oh, I do hope I didn't wake you.

Dorothy No, no. I was just dozing.

Gertrude Oh, I'm absolutely mortified!

Dorothy Oh, don't be silly. Let me make you some coffee.

Gertrude Oh, no, no, no – I'd love to, but there isn't time. I mustn't be late. It's early closing today and I'm the last appointment. Besides, I shall be drowning in lukewarm coffee under the drier.

Dorothy Yes.

Gertrude Now, tell me your news. How's my lovely Victoria?

Dorothy Well, she's . . .

Gertrude Did she like her birthday present?

Dorothy (*brief forgetful moment*) Oh – yes, thank you, Gertrude. That was so sweet of you.

Gertrude Oh, good. I didn't like to send perfume through the post. I thought, if I start her off with a few little charms, then she can collect more as the years go by.

Dorothy Yes, it's a lovely idea.

Gertrude Something to remind her of her dear old godmother. I know young people don't like to send thank-you letters, these days.

Dorothy Sorry, Gertrude.

Gertrude Oh, don't be silly. Did she have a lovely party?

Dorothy Well, she didn't have a party, actually.

Gertrude Oh.

Dorothy She could have had one, if she'd wanted.

Gertrude Yes.

Dorothy But she preferred to stay at home.

Gertrude Oh, that's rather sweet. She wanted to be with Mummy. And how did she get on with her mocks? Brilliantly, I expect.

Dorothy Oh, no – not very well, I'm afraid. She did best in Maths.

Gertrude Oh, good. Clever thing. Though it's hard to know what a girl might do with Maths. Oh – now, when is Edwin's big day?

Dorothy Oh, not long now. In May, just after his birthday.

Gertrude Gosh – so soon. What will he do with himself?

Dorothy Well, I don't know. Read, I expect.

Gertrude He'll be rather under your feet, won't he?

Dorothy I suppose so.

Gertrude Oh, darling! That's not ideal, is it?

Dorothy Well . . .

Gertrude We shall have to find him a hobby. A man can't just sit and read books all day, can he? Now, my dear, I must dash. See what can be done to salvage my locks!

They both get up.

Dorothy How are Cedric and Adele?

Gertrude Oh, well – you know. Cedric is Cedric is Cedric. And Adele is her usual mysterious self. (*Pause.*) Actually, I'm not sure that she wasn't rather poorly yesterday morning, but I daren't ask. I'd get my head bitten off. (*Pause.*) Anyway . . .

She moves off towards the door, but stops to look at the flowers on the sideboard.

Oh, look! Aren't these charming? Beautifully arranged. You're such a clever girl. Very artistic.

Dorothy Thank you.

Gertrude (*seeing photograph*) Ah, dear Victor . . . That is such a striking portrait, isn't it? Do you remember that happy little dinner party I threw to celebrate your engagement?

Dorothy Oh, yes.

Gertrude That was this time of year, wasn't it? Just a few months before war broke out. A lovely, bright, spring evening. We drank champagne on our terrace, and I served my famous vichyssoise, didn't I?

Dorothy Yes.

Gertrude Dear, dear Victor. Such a comical fellow. Had us all in absolute tucks all evening. Yes. A thoroughly decent chap. A man amongst men.

Dorothy starts to cry.

Oh, my dear . . . I'm so sorry. Come and sit down.

Dorothy sits. Gertrude puts down her handbag.

I am such a silly girl. 'Garrulous Gertie'. Oh, my darling – I'm dreadfully sorry.

She puts her hands sympathetically on Dorothy's shoulders.

Dorothy I'm just so tired all the time, Gertrude. And everything seems . . .

Gertrude Seems what, my dear?

Dorothy Oh . . . you know.

Gertrude Yes, I know. (*Pause.*) Still, we must just soldier on, mustn't we? (*Pause.*) Let me fetch you something. How about a nice cup of sweet tea?

Dorothy No, thank you.

Gertrude Would you like a cigarette?

Dorothy Oh, no.

Gertrude I know what you need. A good hot bath. Do you have any bath salts?

Dorothy Yes, I think so.

Gertrude Splendid. A jolly good soak, and you'll be ready to face the world again. Shall I pop upstairs and run it for you?

Dorothy Oh, no, thank you, Gertrude.

She gets up.

Gertrude Are you sure?

Dorothy Yes. I don't want you to miss your hairdressing appointment.

Gertrude Oh, no – of course.

She collects her handbag.

I hate to leave you like this.

Dorothy Oh, it's all right. I'd rather be by myself.

Gertrude Yes. Sometimes that's the best thing, isn't it? Silence and solitude. (*Pause.*) Well, chin up, Headset Forty-Four! Nil desperandum. Try to look on the bright side – things could be much worse, you know.

She opens the door, and stops on the threshold.

I shall give you a ring this evening – will you be in?

Dorothy Yes, I expect so.

Gertrude Splendid.

She strides into the hall. Dorothy follows.

(*Off.*) Now, up you go, and don't stint on the hot water. I mustn't keep Caroline waiting.

The front door opens.

Goodbye, my darling. Now you take very good care, and look after yourself, won't you?

Dorothy (*off*) Yes, I will.

Gertrude (*off*) Bye-bye, my darling. TTFN! Bye-bye.

Gertrude leaves. Dorothy closes the front door. She pauses for a moment at the door, then closes it from the hall.
Fade lights.

A weekday afternoon in late spring.
  Victoria is sitting on the sofa. She is wearing her school uniform. Dorothy enters from the kitchen.

Dorothy The kettle's on. A nice cup of tea, and then perhaps you should go upstairs and try to do a little revision. Oh – don't forget, it's Uncle Edwin's birthday soon. I know you'll want to get him a present. It's so difficult to buy for men, isn't it? You won't forget, will you?

Victoria I can't be bothered.

Dorothy What d'you mean, you can't be bothered?

Victoria I mean, I can't be bothered to buy Uncle Edwin a present.

Dorothy sits down.

Dorothy Well, that's very selfish of you, Victoria. How d'you think he's going to feel about that?

Victoria I'm too busy.

Dorothy Too busy doing what?

Victoria Revising for my 'O'-levels.

Dorothy Well, yes – I think you should start revising. You haven't got long now, but I'm sure you can spare an hour or so.

Pause. Victoria sighs.

Victoria If you want him to have a present from me, you can get it yourself.

She has got up and is leaving the room.

Dorothy No, darling. I'm not doing that.

She gets up, and goes into the hall.

Victoria, please!

Fade lights.

SCENE SIXTEEN

A weekday evening in May. Edwin's birthday.
Dorothy enters from the kitchen. She is wearing her apron. She paces the room, nervously. She picks up an unsealed birthday card in its envelope from an arm of the sofa, and immediately puts it back. There are two wrapped birthday presents with another (sealed) card on the other sofa arm.
A key is heard in the front door. Dorothy goes out into the hall.

Dorothy Oh, hello, dear.

Edwin (*off*) Hello.

Dorothy rushes back into the room, and hurriedly puts the unsealed card into a sideboard drawer. Edwin enters the room. He is wearing his hat and coat.

Dorothy Happy birthday – again!

Edwin Thank you.

He removes his hat.

Dorothy How was your day?

Edwin Oh, well . . . you know.

Dorothy Oh, apron – sorry!

Edwin goes out to hang up his hat and coat, while Dorothy scuttles off to the kitchen to remove her apron. She returns, then he does.

Victoria isn't home yet.

79

Edwin Oh, isn't she?

Dorothy No. Most unusual.

Edwin Yes.

He spots the presents on the sofa.

Oh! Something for me?

Dorothy Of course.

Edwin How lovely.

He sits on the sofa. Dorothy joins him. Edwin moves the presents to the middle of the sofa, and picks up the card.

May I?

Dorothy Oh, yes.

Edwin opens the card and reads it. A key is heard in the front door.

Edwin Oh, Dorothy – thank you.

Dorothy You're welcome. Oh, here she is.

She gets up. Victoria appears in the doorway.

Dorothy Hello, darling. You're late.

Victoria (*coming in*) Happy birthday, Uncle Edwin.

Edwin Thank you, Victoria.

Victoria I'll just put my bag away.

Dorothy Yes.

Victoria goes out. She returns, having taken off her satchel and her school uniform hat. Dorothy joins her.

Uncle Edwin is about to open his presents.

Edwin picks up his presents. Dorothy communicates to Victoria, in rather bad mime, that one of the two presents is 'from' Victoria.

Sit down, dear.

Victoria sits on the sofa, next to Edwin.

Now: this evening, I shall pour our sherries.

Edwin Jolly good.

Dorothy goes over to the sideboard to pour the drinks.

Well, this is exciting.

Victoria Yes. (*Pause.*) Have you had a lovely day?

Edwin Yes, thank you.

Victoria Good.

Dorothy Victoria, would you like a sherry?

Victoria Yes, please, Mummy.

Dorothy completes the pouring, then gives Edwin and Victoria their drinks.

Edwin Thank you.

Victoria Thank you.

Dorothy collects her sherry from the sideboard and joins them.

Dorothy Chin-chin. Happy birthday.

Edwin Chin-chin.

Victoria Happy birthday.

Edwin sips his sherry. Victoria raises hers to her lips, but before she has had a chance to drink, Dorothy speaks . . .

Dorothy Sip it slowly, Victoria. You don't want it to go to your head.

Victoria freezes, then lowers her drink, without taking a sip. Dorothy clocks this for a moment, then sits in the armchair.

Edwin starts to unwrap the smaller of the two presents.

Edwin Now then . . .

Dorothy That's from me. It's a tiepin.

Edwin Oh, Dorothy, it's beautiful.

Dorothy I wasn't sure.

Edwin Oh, you shouldn't have. (*To Victoria.*) Now . . .

He unwraps the second present, which is a box of white handkerchiefs.

Oh, how lovely. With my initial!

Dorothy Yes. Didn't she choose well?

Edwin Oh, she did. Thank you, Victoria. Good girl. (*Pause.*) I'm as happy as a sandboy.

Dorothy smiles. Victoria puts down her glass.

Victoria I have to go upstairs. (*She gets up.*) I hope you have a lovely evening. Happy birthday.

She goes to the door, and heads upstairs.

Dorothy You haven't drunk your sherry, darling.

She gets up and goes to the bottom of the stairs.

Victoria? Dinner will be in about half an hour. Please make sure you come down for Uncle Edwin's birthday, won't you, darling?

*Victoria closes her bedroom door. Dorothy comes
back into the room, and closes the door. She collects
her sherry, pauses for a short while, and joins Edwin
on the sofa. Pause.*

Dorothy A special treat tonight. Steak.

Edwin Ooh.

*Pause. Edwin starts to sing, softly. After a moment,
Dorothy joins in: 'Apple Blossom Time' by Fleeson
and Von Tilzer.*

Edwin (*singing*)
I'll be with you in apple blossom time –

Edwin *and* **Dorothy** (*singing*)
I'll be with you to change your name to mine.
One day in May,
I'll come and say:
'Happy the bride the sun shines on today!'

What a wonderful wedding there will be,
What a wonderful day for you and me!
Church bells will chime,
You will be mine,
In apple blossom time.

*The song ends. Pause Edwin looks at Dorothy. Pause.
Fade lights.*

SCENE SEVENTEEN

*A few days later. Afternoon. May.
    Edwin enters at the front door. He comes into the
living room, and stands contemplatively for a few
moments. He is wearing his hat. His coat is over his arm,
along with his case, his newspaper, his book and a large,
red presentation box.*

Dorothy enters from upstairs.

Dorothy Hello, dear.

Edwin Hello.

Dorothy I heard you come in, I was just . . . upstairs. Well, how was it?

Edwin It's all over, now. (*He removes his hat.*)

Dorothy Yes. (*She pats his arm.*) Yes it is. Brave soldier. Oh, what a lovely box!

Edwin An empty train for once.

Dorothy Oh gosh – of course, you've finally managed to beat the rush hour.

Edwin Just a couple of German tourists.

Dorothy Let me unburden you.

She takes the box.

Edwin Oh, thank you.

Dorothy also takes Edwin's book and newspaper. She puts these on his side table, but holds the box. Edwin hangs up his hat and coat in the hall, then returns.

Dorothy Can I get you something? A cup of tea? Or a whisky, perhaps?

Edwin No, thank you.

He sits on the sofa. Dorothy joins him, resting the box on her knees.

Dorothy Well . . . May I have a look?

Edwin I was late for work this morning.

Dorothy Oh?

Edwin Yes, there was a bit of a kerfuffle at Mortlake.

Dorothy Gosh, what happened?

Edwin Well, the train stood for an inordinate length of time. Absolute silence. Then, suddenly, there was a great deal of shouting, and a big man ran the entire length of the platform, hotly pursued by an even bigger man. We didn't leave for a further five minutes. When we arrived at Waterloo, the ticket barrier was surrounded by policemen. I was twelve minutes late at the office.

Dorothy Oh, you've never been late, have you?

Edwin Not since the Blitz.

Dorothy No. Well, they can't very well sack you, can they?

They laugh.

May I?

Edwin Yes, of course.

She opens the box.

Dorothy Oh, Edwin! What a beautiful salver. Let me get my glasses.

She collects her reading glasses from the table next to her armchair, returns to the sofa, and takes out of the box a round, silver salver.

Oh, lovely. (*Reading.*) 'Presented to Mr E. H. Lavender . . .' (*Pause. She removes her spectacles.*) Oh, Edwin, they've spelt your name incorrectly.

Edwin Yes, I know.

Dorothy Oh, that's dreadful. (*She puts on her spectacles.*)

Edwin It doesn't matter. As they say, it's the thought that counts.

Dorothy removes her glasses.

Dorothy Yes, but you would think somebody might have known. (*Puts on her spectacles, and reads.*) 'Presented to Mr E. H. Lavender . . . on the occasion of his retirement, after forty-five years' sterling service with the Yorkshire Insurance Company, the second of May, 1958.'

She removes her spectacles, puts the salver back in its box, and goes to her armchair. She sits, and takes out a handkerchief from her handbag. She wipes her eyes – the inscription has moved her very slightly to tears.

What did, Mr . . . um, you know – with the funny name. What did he have to say?

Edwin Mr Vienthe? Yes, he made a short speech, thanking me for my forty years' service.

Dorothy But it's been forty-five years.

Edwin Yes, I know, but he apparently labours under the misapprehension that it's been only forty.

Pause. Dorothy joins him on the sofa again.

Dorothy Did you manage to speak to him in private?

Edwin No, he left in rather a hurry. I'm sure he must have had a more important engagement.

Dorothy And did you make your speech?

Edwin I'm afraid so, yes.

Dorothy What did you say?

Edwin (*gesturing*) Oh, you . . .

Were he to finish this sentence, it would probably be something like 'Oh, you don't want to know about that!'
He takes out a piece of paper from his inside pocket, and glances over it. He appears to be about to read it out, but –

I just thanked everybody, really.

He folds up the speech and puts it away. Pause.
Dorothy puts the lid back on the box, having reinstated
the salver earlier.

Dorothy I expect you had a nice lunch with the chaps?

Edwin Oh, yes. Very convivial. A piece of pork pie and
a glass of mild.

Dorothy gets up, holding the salver box.

Dorothy Where would you like this to live?

Edwin Well, I thought perhaps the dining room.

Dorothy Oh, yes – on the sideboard.

Edwin Yes. D'you know, dear, I think perhaps I might
have that whisky, after all.

Dorothy Yes, of course. (*Touching him, gently.*) It's been
an exciting day.

She puts down the box, goes over to the sideboard,
and pours him a whisky. During this, he dozes off. She
returns, and sits next to him.

Edwin, dear . . .

Edwin (*waking*) Oh – I'm sorry.

He takes the whisky.

Thank you.

Dorothy Why don't you have a little afternoon nap?

Edwin What a good idea. Chin-chin.

He gets up.

Dorothy I'll wake you at teatime.

Edwin Thank you.

He goes upstairs. She follows him out, but in the
direction of the dining room.
Fade lights.

SCENE EIGHTEEN

A weekday afternoon. Late May.
   Dorothy is sitting in the armchair, reading a book.
Edwin is on the sofa, reading The Times. *Pause. Dorothy*
takes out her handkerchief, and blows her nose.

Edwin A bit sniffly?

Dorothy Yes, I am. Hay fever.

Edwin That time of year.

   Pause.

Dorothy Yes. It is.

   Pause. They both read.

Edwin Four hundred and seventy-five thousand, six
hundred and eight pounds. That's a lot of money to
leave, isn't it?

Dorothy What, in a will?

Edwin Yes.

   Pause.

Dorothy Yes, it's a great deal of money.

   Pause.

Edwin Oh-oh . . . General de Gaulle.

Dorothy I'm sorry?

Edwin Algeria.

   Pause.

What cake do we have?

Dorothy Madeira.

The doorbell rings, a little excitedly.

Goodness me. Who's that?

She puts down her book. The bell rings again.

Oh!

She answers the door.

(*Off.*) Oh, hello darling.

Victoria (*off, entering*) I forgot my key.

Dorothy (*off, closing the door*) Oh. Would you like some tea?

Victoria (*off, going upstairs*) No.

Dorothy (*coming into the room*) No, '*thank you*', Victoria.

Victoria's bedroom door closes.

Shall we have that tea, then?

Edwin Jolly good.

The doorbell rings again.

Dorothy Oh, goodness me!

She answers the door.

Hugh (*off*) Hello, Dorothy. I just had a few minutes to spare, and I thought I'd see if the old reprobate was at home.

He enters the room, holding his hat. Dorothy follows. Edwin gets up.

Ah, there he is! How are you, old bean? How's tricks in the Land of the Lotus Eaters?

Edwin Oh, not too bad, thank you.

Dorothy I think he's coping with it all – aren't you, dear?

Edwin Of course.

Hugh Jolly good. Frightfully convenient for me, being able to drop in on you like this for a chin-wag in the middle of the week.

Edwin Yes.

Hugh I'm between visits, you know. I have a sciatica in Strawberry Hill.

Dorothy Oh, dear.

Hugh laughs.

Well, I was just about to make some tea. Would you care to join us?

Hugh Oh, no, thank you, Dorothy. I really don't have time today – I'm rushed off my feet.

Dorothy Of course. Well, would you excuse me?

Hugh By all means.

Dorothy exits to the kitchen.

So, how are we?

He hangs his hat on a chair. Edwin returns to the sofa.

Edwin Well, I'm still getting that pain behind the eyes.

Hugh You're reading too much.

Edwin Am I?

Hugh Yes – it can make you go blind, that sort of thing. (*Laughs uproariously.*) You ought to get your eyes tested, get yourself a stronger pair of spectaculars.

Edwin Ah, well perhaps I will.

Hugh joins him on the sofa.

Hugh Guess where my errant son's off to!

Edwin Oh, I really couldn't say.

Hugh Go on – three guesses.

Edwin Well, I don't know. Em . . . abroad somewhere?

Hugh Absolutely. Russia! Moscow and Leningrad.

Edwin Moscow?

Hugh Yes, he's attending a conference on 'cybernetics', whatever that may be. (*He pronounces this 'kybernetics'.*) He did explain, and it went in one ear and out the other. Ethel's worried he might defect. (*Laughs.*) He's popping into Leningrad on the way back. Oh, bit of a change of plan, interestingly. We've decided to go to France in August.

Edwin Oh?

Hugh Yes, we got cold feet about the weather in Norfolk. So, we've settled on a region called the Jura Mountains. Recommended by a patient of mine. Awfully good grub, apparently. It's spelt 'jura', but its pronounced 'yura'.

Edwin 'Yura' – yes.

Dorothy returns. She stands in the doorway.

Hugh I kept saying 'jura', and he said, 'No, no, doctor – it's "yura",' so I said, 'Oh, yolly good!' (*Laughs uproariously.*) He who laughs last thinks slowest! (*Laughs.*) One final fling before the grave! We'll probably expire halfway up a mountain.

He now gets up, and performs a sort of bad caricature mime of puffing and panting up a steep mountain. This erupts into an attack of uncontrolled hysterical mirth. When this is over, he pats Edwin on the knee.

You bearing up all right, though, old bean?

Edwin Yes, thank you.

Hugh Jolly good. Well . . . duty calls. (*He picks up his hat.*) Keep smiling through. I'll see you very soon, old chap. Arrivederci!

Dorothy sees him out.

Dorothy (*off*) Lovely to see you, Hugh.

Hugh (*off*) Very nice to see you, too, Dorothy.

Dorothy (*off*) Give my regards to Ethel.

Hugh (*off*) Of course. Thank you.

Dorothy (*off*) Goodbye.

Hugh (*off*) Goodbye.

Dorothy closes the front door, and returns.

Dorothy (*remembering*) Oh, yes . . .

She goes out to make the tea. Pause.
Fade lights.

SCENE NINETEEN

A weekday morning in June.
Maureen is finishing polishing the parquet floor, using a dry mop. When she reaches the door, she stops, and exits.

Maureen (*off*) That's me finished in there, Mrs Molyneux.

Dorothy (*off*) Thank you, Maureen.

Edwin (*off*) Thank you, Maureen.

Maureen (*off*) No bother.

Edwin (*off*) Thank you very much.

Dorothy and Edwin enter. Dorothy has a magazine and her handbag. She sits in the armchair. Edwin has his newspaper and a lit pipe. He sits on the sofa. Dorothy listens, as Maureen can be heard going upstairs to Victoria's room.

Victoria (*off*) I don't need my room cleaned, thank you.

Maureen (*off*) Your mother wants me to clean the room.

Victoria (*off*) It doesn't need cleaning. It's fine.

Maureen (*off*) Your mother wants it cleaned.

Victoria (*off*) I'd like to be left on my own. Please go away.

Maureen (*off*) You may go and speak to your mother.

Victoria (*off, louder*) Get out of my room.

Maureen (*off*) D'you want me to go downstairs and bring your mother up here?

Victoria (*off, shouting*) I don't care, just get out.

Maureen comes down the stairs, and into the room. Dorothy affects engrossed reading, ostrich-like.

Maureen She won't let me in near the room, Mrs Molyneux. She's neither manners nor breeding, that one.

She stomps off to the kitchen. Victoria rushes down the stairs, and storms into the room. Dorothy gets up.

Victoria Mummy – I don't want her in my room!

Dorothy Darling, it's just for fifteen minutes.

Victoria I don't care. I don't want anyone in my room – it's my room!

Dorothy Yes, I know that, but she has to change the sheets.

Victoria You're not listening to me!

Dorothy Yes, I am listening to you, darling.

Victoria You never listen to me! I just want to be left on my own. That's all I ask.

She rushes upstairs and slams her door. Dorothy goes over to the window. Throughout all of the following, Edwin remains apparently oblivious, continuing to puff on his pipe, and to read.
Maureen enters from the kitchen, dressed in her hat and coat, ready to leave.

Maureen That's me finished, Mrs Molyneux – I've had enough. Give me me money now, and I'll be on my way.

Dorothy You haven't done the kitchen – have you?

Maureen No, and I won't be doing it either. I've had enough of this house.

Dorothy I'm sorry, Maureen.

Maureen She needs a good clip round the ear, that one. I've never been spoken to like that before in my life. (*Pause.*) Give me me money now, and we'll leave it at that.

Dorothy takes out her purse, and gives Maureen a ten-shilling note.

Dorothy I'm so sorry, Maureen . . .

Maureen Good luck to you.

She goes out. Dorothy follows.

Dorothy (*off*) Goodbye.

She closes the front door. She returns, and stands in the doorway. Edwin continues to read and smoke. She considers him for a while, then exits to the kitchen.
Fade lights.

SCENE TWENTY

A weekday morning. Late August.
 Dorothy is standing, looking out of the window.
Edwin is sitting on the sofa, reading the newspaper.
Dorothy starts to pace round the room.

Dorothy I wonder what's happened to her. She should have been back by now.

She stops and looks at Edwin. No response. She moves off. The key is heard in the front door.

Here she is.

The front door closes. Dorothy goes to the doorway of the room.

Hello, darling.

Victoria enters, carrying her satchel. She sits on the sofa. Edwin puts down his newspaper.

What's the news?

Victoria What d'you think?

Dorothy I don't know. That's what we're waiting to hear.

She sits down.

Victoria I failed.

Pause.

Dorothy What d'you mean, you failed?

Victoria I failed my 'O'-levels.

Pause.

Dorothy What, all of them?

Victoria Yes.

Dorothy Even Maths?

Victoria I didn't take Maths.

Dorothy What d'you mean, you didn't take Maths?

Victoria I mean, I didn't go to the exam.

Dorothy Why ever not? It's your best subject.

Victoria Who says?

Pause.

Dorothy Well, isn't it?

Pause. Then Victoria shrugs.

How many other examinations did you miss?

Victoria Two. French and Latin.

Pause.

Dorothy So, how many did you take?

Victoria Four, obviously.

Pause.

Dorothy Victoria, I don't know what to say.

Victoria Don't say anything. It doesn't matter. Nothing matters.

She goes up to her room. Her bedroom door closes. Edwin has returned to his newspaper. Long pause.

Edwin Disappointing.

Pause.

Dorothy Aren't you going to take your little walk, this morning?

Edwin Oh, yes. (*Puts down his newspaper.*) Perhaps I will.

He exits, swapping his spectacles as he goes. He leaves through the front door.

Dorothy reflects for a few moments. Then she goes over to the sofa, adjusts a cushion, and half lies down. Pause.

Fade lights.

SCENE TWENTY-ONE

Evening. September.

Edwin comes in. He goes to the sideboard, and starts to pour two sherries. Dorothy enters, closes the door, and goes over to the window, where she closes the curtains. As she passes Edwin, he begins to sing 'Night and Day' by Cole Porter.

Edwin (*singing*)
Night and day, you are the one.
Only you, beneath the moon and under the sun.
Whether near to me, or far,
No matter, darling, where you are,
I think of you, night and day.

Dorothy lights a cigarette. Then she takes her sherry from Edwin and sits in the armchair.

Day and night, why is it so,
That this longing for you
Foll . . . (*He trails off.*)

Pause. He looks sideways, over his shoulder, in Dorothy's direction, but not at her. She glances at him briefly. He sits on the sofa. Pause.

Chin-chin.

Dorothy Chin-chin.

They each take a sip. He swaps his spectacles for his reading glasses. He opens his book, and starts to read. Long pause.

The door opens very slowly. Victoria enters, equally slowly. She is wearing pyjamas, and her hair is slightly dishevelled. She is preoccupied, almost as though sleepwalking, but not actually.

Hello, darling.

Victoria says nothing. She moves to the back of the sofa, and stands for a moment, stroking it. Edwin is reading his book, and is taking no notice of her.

Are you all right?

Pause. Victoria turns, and moves silently out of the room, leaving the door open. She goes back upstairs.

Victoria?

Dorothy puts down her cigarette, gets up and follows Victoria upstairs. Pause, Victoria's door can be heard closing, gently. Dorothy returns to the room, and closes the door. Edwin remains absorbed in his book.

She's just a little tired.

Pause.

Edwin Is she?

Pause. Dorothy picks up her cigarette, and smokes it. She remains standing. She reflects for a while.

Dorothy I'll go and prepare dinner.

She walks towards the door.

Edwin (*not looking up*) Jolly good.

Dorothy pauses and looks at Edwin. Then she goes out, closing the door. Edwin reads. Pause. Fade lights.

SCENE TWENTY-TWO

Late morning. September.

Edwin is sitting on the sofa, reading another book.
Dorothy is standing at the window. Pause. Dorothy drifts
around the room. She looks tired. She stops for a moment
at Victor's photograph. Then she moves round Edwin on
the sofa.

Dorothy I must try to find another cleaner.

Edwin (*looking up*) For whom?

Dorothy For us, of course.

Edwin But we each have one.

Dorothy Each have what?

Edwin A key.

Dorothy (*irritated*) No, Edwin. I said, a cleaner.

Edwin Oh.

Dorothy I need to find one.

Edwin Yes. I think you should.

He returns to his book. Dorothy sits in the armchair.
She puts on her reading glasses.
The doorbell rings. Dorothy looks at Edwin. He
carries on reading. She gets up and goes to answer the
door.

Muriel (*off*) Ta-da!

Gertrude (*off*) Hello, my dear Dorothy!

Dorothy (*off*) Goodness me!

Gertrude (*off*) Oh, do forgive us – we're being very, very,
very wicked ladies!

She comes into the room. Edwin has put his book down, and is standing. Muriel and Dorothy talk in the hall, just outside the doorway. This overlaps with Gertrude's line to Edwin.

Muriel *(off)* We wanted to surprise you.

Dorothy *(off)* Yes, well you have! Do go in.

Gertrude Oh, Edwin! What a surprise! Of course, you're a gentleman of leisure these days, aren't you?

Muriel and Dorothy come in.

Edwin I'm afraid so, yes.

Muriel Hello, Edwin.

Edwin Hello, Muriel.

Gertrude And how are you enjoying your retirement?

Edwin Oh, very nice, thank you.

Gertrude Oh, I'm so pleased.

Dorothy Would you like some coffee?

Muriel No, thank you . . .

Gertrude Absolutely not!

Muriel Edwin, we've come to kidnap your sister.

Gertrude Quite legally, of course!

She sits on the sofa.

(*To Edwin.*) Do sit down, my dear.

Edwin sits next to Gertrude.

Muriel *(indicating chair)* May I?

Dorothy Oh, yes, of course!

Muriel moves the chair and sits in it. Dorothy sits in the armchair.

Gertrude No, we've just had a lovely morning. We started off with coffees at the Copper Kettle –

Muriel Yes, and I had one of their famous –

Gertrude Muriel indulged in a madeleine, which I managed to resist –

Muriel It was delicious –

Gertrude – and then we popped round the corner and spent a glorious hour rummaging in Partridge's.

Muriel Oh – it was my first visit! I can't believe I've never been there before.

Gertrude I know – isn't that extraordinary?

Muriel Yes, and I bought the most beautiful –

Gertrude Oh, and Muriel found some stunning olive duchess satin, didn't you, darling?

Muriel Yes, I did. I'm going to have it made up into a cocktail dress for Paris – Of course, you don't know: Gerald is going to treat me to a weekend in Paris to make up for our frightful holiday –

Gertrude (*Simultaneously.*) Edwin, do forgive all this 'girls' talk'. Simply close your ears, my dear. (*Continuing.*) Of course! You haven't heard about Muriel's disaster –

Muriel No, I was just about to tell –

Gertrude Dear Gerald was struck down by a nasty little summer cold, so the poor things had to curtail their holiday and fly home four days early in tourist class, didn't you?

Muriel Yes, imagine –

Gertrude Well, of course, we've just come back from Cannes, as you know. Absolutely lovely – terribly handsome waiters, although I'm not sure that one should take one's holiday in the same place too many times.

Muriel Well, it can be disappointing, can't it?

Gertrude Well, yes, it *can*. But not necessarily.

Pause.

Muriel Oh – your holiday! Where did you go in the end?

Dorothy Well, we didn't go anywhere, actually.

Gertrude Oh, Dorothy! You are such a naughty girl!

Muriel Now, what did we tell you?

Gertrude (*to Edwin*) I think you should insist on taking your sister somewhere exotic next year. It would do her so much good, you know.

Muriel It would do you all good.

Gertrude (*to Edwin*) Bermuda. Or Capri.

Dorothy Well, it was a little difficult this summer.

Gertrude In what way?

Muriel (*simultaneously*) Oh, why?

Dorothy Well . . . Victoria's 'O'-levels . . .

Gertrude Oh, gosh! My darling – how did she get on?

Muriel (*simultaneously*) Victoria! Of course.

Dorothy Not very well, I'm afraid.

Gertrude Oh, dear –

Muriel (*simultaneously*) Oh.

Gertrude – how disappointing for her, and she worked so terribly hard, didn't she?

Muriel Yes. I'm sure she did her best.

Gertrude I don't think it makes too much difference, in the long run, just so long as she's happy.

Muriel Yes. Is she back at school?

Dorothy No. (*Pause.*) She's upstairs.

Gertrude Oh!

Muriel Might we see her?

Dorothy Oh . . . Well, er, yes . . . I expect she'll be down soon.

Muriel Oh, good. It's ages since I've seen my goddaughter.

Gertrude (*simultaneously*) Oh, marvellous. Always a treat to see my lovely goddaughter. (*She continues.*) So – there we were, coming out of Partridge's – they're such a marvellous shop, you know. (*To Edwin.*) Nothing's too much trouble for them – they're quite heroic. They'll always order you even the tiniest piece of fabric. (*To Dorothy.*) And we were planning to drive up to the West End –

Muriel Oh, yes –

Gertrude – but it suddenly struck me, and I said to Muriel, our dear friend Dorothy is only ten minutes away, sitting at home, twiddling her thumbs. Why don't we pick her up, and whisk her off for a jolly lunch at the dear old White Hart Hotel?

Muriel How about that?

Dorothy Oh. I'm not sure . . .

Muriel Well, we *are* sure, aren't we, Gertrude?

Gertrude Oh, most definitely. And we shan't take no for an answer, shall we?

Muriel No.

Dorothy Oh, goodness me . . . I'm not really suitably dressed . . .

Muriel Oh, that doesn't matter.

Gertrude Oh, my darling – don't be silly! Neither are we. Look at me: I bought this last year!

Dorothy It is very kind of you both . . .

Muriel Oh, kindness has nothing to do with it. We want our Headset Forty-Four.

Gertrude Yes, it wouldn't be the same without you.

Muriel No.

Dorothy Who's going to serve Edwin his lunch?

Gertrude Oh, he'll manage. (*To Edwin.*) You chaps usually can, can't you, when push comes to shove?

Muriel Yes.

Gertrude 'Needs must when the Devil drives'.

Edwin I'll be fine.

Gertrude Of course you will.

Dorothy Are you sure?

Edwin Oh, yes.

Muriel There.

Gertrude Splendid.

Dorothy There's a piece of pork pie in the fridge.

Edwin Lovely.

Gertrude Good. Well – ready when you are.

Dorothy Er, yes. Well, um . . .

Gertrude Why don't you pop upstairs, put a face on, and then we'll be off?

Dorothy Yes . . . Well, I won't be a minute.

Muriel There's our girl.

Gertrude 'Put on your shoes, we're going to have some fun!' I'm absolutely famished.

Dorothy goes upstairs.

Muriel Success!

Gertrude Absolutely. Not hard at all.

Muriel No.

Gertrude (*to Edwin*) I expect you'll be glad of some peace and quiet, won't you, Edwin?

Edwin Oh . . .

Gertrude It's so nice to see you still smoking your pipe. I do like a man with a pipe. (*To Muriel.*) Of course, Gerald's a great pipe man, isn't he?

Muriel He is, indeed.

Gertrude Interestingly, Cedric never has been.

Muriel No. He likes a cigar, doesn't he?

Gertrude Yes, occasionally. (*To Edwin.*) How about you, Edwin? Do you enjoy a cigar from time to time?

Edwin Rather wasted on me, I'm afraid.

Gertrude Oh really? I always think there's something terribly magnetic about a man with a cigar.

Muriel Mmm, I love the smell.

Gertrude Absolutely. Reminds me of poor, dear Daddy.

Muriel Oh, Gertrude.

Gertrude So, how are you filling in your days now that you've retired?

Edwin Ah, well . . .

Gertrude You must be missing your work chums, I expect?

Edwin Oh, I don't know . . .

Gertrude Or perhaps there are one or two of them you're not altogether sorry to see the back of?

Edwin laughs.

You wicked man! Well, of course, Cedric used to talk incessantly about taking early retirement, but I'm glad to say I've finally dissuaded him. One hears these terrible stories about perfectly healthy men; they retire, and before you know it, they've keeled over, and popped their clogs!

Muriel laughs. So does Gertrude. Dorothy returns, wearing a hat and coat, and having made up her face.

Muriel Oh, here she is.

Gertrude Oh, my darling! You look absolutely sweet.

Dorothy Thank you. I'll just get my handbag.

She collects it from near the armchair.

Gertrude Good. Then we'll be off.

Gertrude and Muriel start to put on their gloves.

Muriel Now, you've a hankering for a lamp chop, haven't you?

Gertrude Oh, yes, indeed, my darling – if not several.

Muriel I was thinking of a lemon sole.

Gertrude Oh, yes – lovely.

Dorothy I think I'll just pop upstairs, and say goodbye to Victoria.

Gertrude Oh, good. Well, do give her our best, won't you?

Muriel Oh, yes.

Dorothy goes upstairs.

Gertrude Ah, dear Victoria.

Muriel Yes. Perhaps we'll see her later.

Gertrude Yes. Well, Edwin, I do hope it's not too long before we meet again.

Edwin I pray not.

Gertrude It's been so lovely to have a little chat and catch up.

Muriel Yes.

Edwin Indeed.

Gertrude I expect you're looking forward to a jolly good snooze after lunch, aren't you? I can't say I blame you. (*To Muriel.*) Well, my dear – ready for the off?

Muriel Rather.

Some bangs from upstairs, then Dorothy shouting.

Dorothy (*off*) Victoria! Victoria!!

Gertrude and Muriel stop and listen. Dorothy can be heard rushing on to the landing.

(*Off, shouting hysterically.*) Edwin!!

Gertrude and Muriel look at each other. Gertrude looks at Edwin. He doesn't move. From this point, dramatic music underpins the action.

Muriel (*getting up*) Dorothy? What's the matter? Dorothy!

Gertrude (*getting up*) Oh, my God . . .

Muriel and Gertrude rush out of the room and go upstairs to Victoria's room. Edwin remains frozen on the sofa, and so remains until the end of the play.

The following dialogue, mixed in, as it is, with the score, need not be heard precisely and with great clarity. The mood of panic and mayhem is more important.

Dorothy (*off*) Victoria, darling – please! Victoria, speak to me . . .

Muriel (*off*) Dorothy?

Gertrude (*off*) Dorothy – what is it?

Dorothy (*off*) Ring for an ambulance!

Muriel (*off*) Gertrude! Ring for an ambulance! It's Victoria!

Dorothy (*off*) Please, Muriel – please go away!

Muriel (*off*) I can't leave you.

Gertrude comes downstairs to the telephone in the hall. She picks up the receiver, but immediately throws it down. She rushes into the room, and heads for her handbag, which is on the sofa next to Edwin.

Gertrude Glasses! My glasses. Where are my glasses? (*She fumbles in her handbag.*) Come on, come on . . .!

She finds them.

Edwin! Don't just sit there, man! Get upstairs!

Edwin doesn't move.

Edwin! Please!

The doorbell rings.

What's the matter with you? (*To herself.*) There's someone at the door.

She opens the front door.

(*Off.*) Oh – Hugh!

Hugh (*off*) Hello, Mrs Wallace.

Gertrude (*off*) Thank heavens!

Hugh (*off*) I had a few minutes to spare, and I just thought I'd see how Edwin was getting on.

Hugh enters the room, removing his hat.

Hello, old bean! How are you?

No response from Edwin. Gertrude has rushed into the room with Hugh.

Gertrude No, no, no, no, my dear – come upstairs! It's Victoria!

Hugh What's the matter with her?

Muriel has rushed downstairs, and enters the room.

Gertrude Oh, poor Dorothy!

Muriel (*simultaneously*) Oh, Hugh – thank God! Upstairs! Quickly!

Gertrude and Muriel bustle Hugh out of the room, and up the stairs. Hugh looks over his shoulder at Edwin as he goes.

Hugh Is she ill?

Muriel Yes! Quickly – they're in her room.

Gertrude (*simultaneously*) It's terrible.

Hugh (*off*) Where is that?

Gertrude (*off*) Muriel, can you ring for an ambulance?

Muriel (*off*) Have you dialled?

Gertrude (*off*) Yes, of course! Oh, no – no, I haven't yet. (*To Hugh.*) It's just round to the right.

Muriel is now in the hall at the telephone. She is dialling.
The following lines from Victoria's bedroom cannot really be heard. Muriel, in the hall on the telephone, is of course loud and clear.

Hugh (*off*) Dorothy, it's Hugh, my dear. It's Hugh.

Muriel (*on phone*) Oh, come *on* . . . !

Gertrude (*off*) Come on, my darling. Let Hugh do what he needs to do.

Dorothy (*off*) Victoria! What's the matter with her, Hugh? Gertrude – please leave me alone!

Gertrude (*off*) All right, my dear. It's all right.

Muriel (*looking round*) EDWIN!

Edwin doesn't react.

(*To operator.*) Hello? Yes, ambulance, please . . .

The music stops. Muriel freezes. Edwin remains frozen. Pause. Then Dorothy utters a loud, wailing, painful, devastating scream . . .

Dorothy No!! VICTORIA!! VICTORIA!! NO!! NO!!

Pause.
Blackout.